SELLING FOLK MUSIC

American Made Music Series

American Made Music Series
Advisory Board

David Evans, General Editor
Barry Jean Ancelet
Edward A. Berlin
Joyce J. Bolden
Rob Bowman
Susan C. Cook
Curtis Ellison
William Ferris
John Edward Hasse
Kip Lornell
Bill Malone
Eddie S. Meadows
Manuel H. Peña
Wayne D. Shirley
Robert Walser

SELLING FOLK MUSIC

AN ILLUSTRATED HISTORY

RONALD D. COHEN AND DAVID BONNER

University Press of Mississippi • Jackson

www.upress.state.ms.us

Designed by Kelly Blanscet/Graphic Granola
and Peter D. Halverson

The University Press of Mississippi is a member of the Association
of American University Presses.

Copyright © 2018 by University Press of Mississippi
All rights reserved

First printing 2018

∞

Library of Congress Cataloging-in-Publication Data

Names: Cohen, Ronald D., 1940– author. | Bonner, David, 1964– author. | Cohen, Ronald D., 1940– Rainbow quest. | Cohen, Ronald D., 1940– Folk music.
Title: Selling folk music : an illustrated history / Ronald D. Cohen and David Bonner.
Description: Jackson : University Press of Mississippi, 2018. | Series: American made music series | "This book is partially meant to be a visual companion to Ronald D. Cohen, Rainbow Quest: The Folk Music Revival and American Society, 1940–1970 (Amherst: University of Massachusetts Press, 2002) and his Folk Music: The Basics (New York: Routledge, 2006)"— Introduction. | Includes bibliographical references and index. |
Identifiers: LCCN 2017015726 (print) | LCCN 2017019443 (ebook) |
ISBN 9781626745841 (epub single) | ISBN 9781626745858 (epub institutional) |
ISBN 9781626745872 (pdf single) | ISBN 9781626745889 (pdf institutional) |
ISBN 9781628462159 (hardcover : alk. paper) | ISBN 9781626745865 (mobi)
Subjects: LCSH: Folk music—United States—History and criticism. | Popular music—United States—History and criticism. | Music trade—United States—History. | Sheet music—United States—History.
Classification: LCC ML3551 (ebook) | LCC ML3551 .C584 2018 (print) | DDC 781.62/13009—dc23
LC record available at https://lccn.loc.gov/2017015726

British Library Cataloging-in-Publication Data available

SPECIAL ACKNOWLEDGMENTS TO THE FOLLOWING:

The Kingston Trio Legacy Project

The Grammy Museum at L.A. Live

The Woody Guthrie Center in Tulsa, Oklahoma

INTRODUCTION

Selling Folk Music is designed to present the public face of folk music in the United States through its commercial promotion and presentation during much of the twentieth century. By "commercial," we mean the ways that folk music was marketed to potential buyers. Of course, throughout history folk songs and folklore have been generally passed down through oral traditions, with their primary impact being their meaning within the local community. "Continuity of past and present is not peculiar to American music but is an important part of it," the *Disc* record catalog explained in 1946. "The roots are as varied as our backgrounds.... The youth, courage and stamina of the nation are present in its songs, as are its mixture of races, its pioneering towards new frontiers—the Erie Canal, the railroads, the songs of steel and cotton, the saga of the cowhands of the west. These are the songs that, like grass roots, have nurtured our musical soil, from folksong and popular song to concert music."

Selling folk music is hardly a modern invention, as songs and ballads have been distributed and popularized at least as far back as the Middle Ages in the British Isles and elsewhere. Folk music has been traditionally defined by scholars as music from a vernacular (or common), nonliterate culture, with anonymous authorship, fairly simple composition, and passed down through oral transmission. It is often understood as music of, by, and for the people, frequently with deep connections to communities defined in ways that may involve affiliations such as regional, ethnic, racial, religious, vocational, and occupational pursuits (cowboys, lumberjacks, miners, sailors, printers, etc.), or other ties.

In the early twentieth century, various collectors, drawing upon earlier publications, such as *Slave Songs of the United States* (1867), began their efforts to document folk songs and ballads in the country. Starting particularly with the British scholar Cecil Sharp and the Texas-based collector John Lomax, they assembled their compilations through vigorous and determined fieldwork, first using written notes, and later employing recording machines to capture the words as well as the music. For example, Carl Sandburg collected songs while touring the country doing poetry readings in the 1920s, while John and Alan Lomax scoured the South in the 1930s for both white and black musicians who had unique repertoires; Alan also did fieldwork in the North. The Lomaxes deposited their recordings in the Archive of American Folk Song at the Library of Congress, which had been launched in 1928 by Robert Winslow Gordon. They were joined by scores of others throughout the country, particularly after Alan became Assistant in Charge of the collection in 1937. Their recordings had no commercial value, until the songs might be published or included in the recordings of others; some, such as those by Lead Belly and Muddy Waters, were first recorded by the Library of Congress. Some collectors based their books on their field recordings, but others used them to document academic articles. Every section of the country has contained traditional songs, in many languages, resulting in a wealth of tunes that would long fascinate folklorists and other collectors. The Library of Congress issued a number of albums in the 1940s edited by Alan Lomax, B. A. Botkin, and others, drawn from their field recordings, in the series "Folk Music of the United States."[1]

While folk music has always had local and communal roots, it has also long had a commercial aspect, often deliberately produced and marketed. Broadsides—single sheets with the printed words on one side and no music—appeared in the British Isles soon after the invention of the printing press in the late fifteenth century. They were designed to be sold, a business for those writing and hawking these sheets, which often commented on local events. There were also published song collections, beginning in the late fifteenth century and significantly increasing in number by the eighteenth century. Folk music has included both ballads (story songs) and pieces featuring a series of perhaps rhyming lyrics, but with no story. The latter might relate to work experiences, life and death, personal relationships, patriotic feelings, or children's games, in a religious or secular context.

By the early years of the twentieth century, folk music, however defined, was widespread in the US, and shared the musical landscape with popular songs professionally written and distributed through sheet music, songbooks, piano rolls, and records, as well as performed on the stage and later in films, as well as radio and television programs. Folk music in the United States—mostly based on Anglo-Saxon and African roots, but also including numerous ethnic styles and sources from throughout the world—has had a varied and complex scope and lineage, including the blues, minstrel tunes, Victorian parlor songs, spirituals and gospel tunes, hillbilly/country/cowboy/western songs, sea shanties, labor and political songs, calypsos, pop folk, folk-rock, ethnic, bluegrass, and a range of so much more.[2]

Broadsides were common in the colonies by the time of the American Revolution, proliferating throughout the United States in the nineteenth century, when they were joined by scores of smaller songsters—collections dealing with a specific topic, such as a political campaign or wartime themes. These songs, part of the marketplace and written for both commercial and political reasons, often entered the folk mainstream and continued to be sung for generations by people unaware of their sources. Larger songbooks began to appear, particularly in the twentieth century, including compilations of folk songs and dances from throughout the country, beginning with Carl Sandburg's *The American Songbag* (1927). Sandburg's influential volume, which remains in print in the twenty-first century, was soon followed by John and Alan Lomax's important *American Ballads and Folk Songs* (1934) and *Our Singing Country* (1941). By the 1930s, there were scores of specialized songbooks, covering various types and styles of ballads and folk songs from throughout the country, and heavily based on field recordings.[3]

When the leading US record companies turned to race and hillbilly recordings after World War I, rural performers both black and white, and primarily from the South, hoped to reap the often-elusive rewards of commercial fame. Since the 1890s, a plethora of folk-related recordings had appeared, representing various racial and ethnic groups. "By early 1920, the national music industry had developed a number of models for selling to the American public," Karl Hagstrom Miller has deftly argued. "It had perfected the mass production of sentimental ballads to pull on the heartstrings of consumers across the nation. It had sold stylized black music in the form of coon songs, Negro dialect ditties, and blues numbers to audiences both black and white. It had featured wisecracking hillbillies in the big city and fiddle breakdowns to entertain urban audiences pining for a taste of the backwoods. And it had learned to expand into new geographical areas by employing native singers to cater to local racial or ethnic markets." Backwoods southern white musicians began to rush into the recording studios following the Texans Eck Robertson and Henry Gilliland's trip to Victor in 1922; Henry Whitter from Virginia and many others followed. Blues musicians also recognized the financial and social appeal of commercial recordings. Record companies depended on the materialistic aspirations of the vernacular musicians, whose songs appeared not only on records but in a profusion of song folios and sheet music.[4]

Following World War II, folk-inspired, urban-based folk musicians who depended on professional careers, many of whom should be noted not as folk singers with traditional, rural roots, but as singers of folk songs—such as Burl Ives, Josh White, Richard Dyer-Bennet, Pete Seeger (who always made this distinction), Susan Reed, and John Jacob Niles—began to appear on records and concert stages. The Weavers had hit records in the early 1950s, and for the remainder of the decade folk music would have some commercial appeal until the phenomenal success of the Kingston Trio beginning in 1958, which kicked off a major commercial folk boom. Records—beginning with 78 rpm single discs and cylinder recordings by the turn of the century, then albums in the 1930s, and 33 1/3 rpm LP albums and 45 rpm singles by the early 1950s—gradually spread folk music across the country. A cascade of promotional products followed by the early 1960s, including magazines, sheet music, concert flyers, paperback books, and posters.

Various critics and folklorists, even John and Alan Lomax, questioned such commercial success, feeling it strayed from the purity and authenticity that they cherished. Since folk music long had a business aspect, however, except for the field recordings that filled the shelves of the Archive of American Folk Song at the Library of Congress and other collections, it was difficult to define what authenticity was all about. Authenticity would generally mean songs with a grassroots lineage, but this has gotten considerably watered down, since what constituted folk songs and ballads has often drawn upon Civil War creations, Victorian parlor songs, early Tin Pan Alley tunes, political and labor union songs, and especially the musical creations of Woody Guthrie, Bob Dylan, Pete Seeger, Phil Ochs, and so many other singer-songwriters. Authenticity has no fixed meaning, so the debate still continues. We take a broad view of the subject, avoiding any strict or narrow interpretation.[5]

We have chosen illustrations from a large variety of commercial sources to encompass how folk music has been packaged and sold to a broad, shifting audience in the United States for much of the twentieth century. We have included concert flyers; covers from sheet music, books, songbooks, magazines, and record albums; concert posters and flyers; movie lobby cards and posters; and a range of commercial products, all in their original colors. The hootenanny craze of 1964, for example, spawned such items as a candy bar, pinball machine, bath powder, paper dolls, Halloween costumes, and beach towels. Such a wide range of images will give a broad and complex picture of the impact that folk music and folk musicians had in transforming public styles and scope into the 1970s. We should note that our decision to end the period covered in this book in the early 1970s was an arbitrary one, reflecting the constraints on the size of the book more than anything else. Commercialized expressions of folk music, such as folk songbooks, recordings, posters, flyers, and much else, have continued to appear into the twenty-first century, and have had an impact on the larger culture. Perhaps a future book will present documentation of that continuing process.

Selling Folk Music is divided into three sections, which are roughly chronological, covering the years 1900–1970. The first section spans the first four decades of the century, including illustrations from songbook covers, sheet music, concert programs, festival flyers, song folios, record album covers, and record company promotional flyers. The second section, roughly including the years 1940–1960, includes the same sorts of materials, with an increasing focus on folk as well as popular magazine covers, concert programs and flyers, and festival programs. The third section, focusing on the 1960s, highlights the popular aspects of folk music during the height of the folk music revival, when protest songs took central stage, followed by the advent of folk-rock, including numerous magazine covers, movie posters and ads, hootenanny commercial products, comic book stories, as well as the proliferating sheet music, book, and songbook covers. These illustrations present a vivid summary of the vibrant commercial nature of folk music over the course of much of the twentieth century. Identifying information is provided for each illustration.

This book is partially meant to be a visual companion to Ronald D. Cohen, *Rainbow Quest: The Folk Music Revival and American Society, 1940–1970* (Amherst: University of Massachusetts Press, 2002) and his *Folk Music: The Basics* (New York: Routledge, 2006), which also includes a lengthy bibliography, although now dated, for those interested in pursuing the history of folk music in the United States (and Great Britain). There are numerous recent studies, which mainly focus on the pre-1970 period, including Dick Weissman, *Which Side Are You On? An Inside History of the Folk Music Revival in America* (2005); Robert Santelli, Holly George-Warren, Jim Brown, eds., *American Roots Music* (2001, with wonderful photos and other illustrations); Michael Scully, *The Never-Ending Revival: Rounder Records and the Folk Alliance* (2008); John Szwed, *Alan Lomax: The Man Who Recorded the World* (2010); Bill Malone, *Music from the True Vine: Mike Seeger's Life and Musical Journey* (2011); David King Dunaway and Holly Beer, *Singing Out: An Oral History of America's Folk Music Revivals* (2010); William G. Roy, *Reds, Whites, and Blues: Social Movements, Folk Music, and Race in the United States* (2010); Bob Riesman, *I Feel So Good: The Life and Times of Big Bill Broonzy* (2011); Will Kaufman, *Woody Guthrie: American Radical* (2011); Richard Carlin, *Worlds of Sound: The Story of Smithsonian Folkways* (2008); Ray Allen, *Gone to the Country: The New Lost City Ramblers and the Folk Music Revival* (2010); Bob Coltman, *Paul Clayton and the Folksong Revival* (2008); David King Dunaway, *How Can I Keep from Singing? The Ballad of Pete Seeger* (2008); Paul O. Jenkins, *Richard Dyer-Bennet: The Last Minstrel* (2010); Philip R. Ratcliffe, *Mississippi John Hurt: His Life, His Times, His Blues* (2011); Daniel Beaumont, *Preachin' the Blues: The Life and Times of Son House* (2011); Ronald D. Cohen, *A History of Folk Music*

Festivals in the United States (2008); Ron Pen, *I Wonder as I Wander: The Life of John Jacob Niles* (2010); Ronald D. Cohen, *Work and Sing: A History of Occupational and Labor Union Songs in the United States* (2010); Hank Reineke, *Arlo Guthrie: The Warner/Reprise Years* (2012); Hank Reineke, *Ramblin' Jack Elliott: The Never-Ending Highway* (2009); Dick Weissman, *Talkin' 'Bout a Revolution: Music and Social Change in America* (2010); Robert Santelli, *This Land Is Your Land: Woody Guthrie and the Journey of an American Folksong* (2012); William J. Bush, *Greenback Dollar: The Incredible Rise of the Kingston Trio* (2013); Scott Barretta, ed., *The Conscience of the Folk Revival: The Writings of Israel "Izzy" Young* (2013); Bruce Conforth, *African American Folksong and American Cultural Politics: The Lawrence Gellert Story* (2013); Ronald D. Cohen and Jim Capaldi, eds., *The Pete Seeger Reader* (2014); Ronald D. Cohen and Rachel Donaldson, *Roots of the Revival: American and British Folk Music in the 1950s* (2014); Ronald D. Cohen and Will Kaufman, *Singing for Peace: Antiwar Songs in American History* (2014); and Stephen Petrus and Ronald D. Cohen's *Folk City: New York and the American Folk Music Revival* (2015).

We include no photos of performers other than those appearing in commercial products. For such photos consult, in particular, David Gahr and Robert Shelton, *The Face of Folk Music* (1968); and Ronald D. Cohen and Bob Riesman, *Chicago Folk: Images of the Sixties Music Scene: The Photographs of Raeburn Flerlage* (2009).

We would like to acknowledge the valuable assistance of Bob Riesman, Kip Lornell, and David Evans. Our special thanks go to Bob Santelli, Executive Director of the Grammy Museum in Los Angeles, and Leslie Reynolds, President of the Board of the Kingston Trio Legacy Foundation, for their support.

RONALD D. COHEN
DAVID BONNER
February 2017

NOTES

1. Ronald D. Cohen, *Alan Lomax, Assistant in Charge: The Library of Congress Letters, 1935–1945* (Jackson: University Press of Mississippi, 2011); Scott B. Spencer, ed., *The Ballad Collectors of North America: How Gathering Folksongs Transformed Academic Thought and American Identity* (Lanham: Scarecrow Press, 2012); and for collectors in the Upper Midwest, James P. Leary, *Polkabilly: How the Goose Island Ramblers Redefined American Folk Music* (New York: Oxford University Press, 2006). For a wonderful discussion of the Library of Congress recordings, see Stephen Wade, *The Beautiful Music All Around Us: Field Recordings and the American Experience* (Urbana: University of Illinois Press, 2012). The original 1940s Library of Congress records were reissued as LPs and then on CDs by Rounder Records.

2. Kip Lornell, *The NPR Curious Listener's Guide to American Folk Music* (New York: Grand Central Press Book, 2004); Lornell, *Introducing American Folk Music* (Madison, WI: Brown & Benchmark, 1993), updated as *Exploring American Folk Music: Ethnic, Grassroots, and Regional Traditions in the United States* (Jackson: University Press of Mississippi, 2012); Stephanie P. Ledgin, *Discovering Folk Music* (Santa Barbara, CA: Praeger, 2010), which includes a selection of photographs; Norm Cohen, *American Folk Songs: A Regional Encyclopedia*, 2 vols. (Westport: Greenwood Press, 2008); Norm Cohen, ed., *Ethnic and Border Music: A Regional Exploration* (Westport: Greenwood Press, 2007); Norm Cohen, *Folk Music: A Regional Exploration* (Westport: Greenwood Press, 2005); and Dick Weissman, *100 Books Every Folk Music Fan Should Own* (Lanham, MD: Rowan and Littlefield, 2014).

3. D. K. Wilgus, *Anglo-American Folksong Scholarship Since 1898* (New Brunswick: Rutgers University Press, 1959); and Spencer, ed., *The Ballad Collectors of North America*.

4. Karl Hagstrom Miller, *Segregating Sound: Inventing Folk and Pop Music in the Age of Jim Crow* (Durham: Duke University Press, 2010), 187, and chap. 6 in general; Patrick Huber, *Linthead Stomp: The Creation of Country Music in the Piedmont South* (Chapel Hill: University of North Carolina Press, 2008); Elijah Wald, *Escaping the Delta: Robert Johnson and the Invention of the Blues* (New York: Amistad, 2004); Marybeth Hamilton, *In Search of the Blues: Black Voices, White Visions* (London: Jonathan Cape, 2007); and the wonderfully illustrated Richard Carlin, *Country Music: The People, Places, and Moments That Shaped the Country Sound* (New York: Black Dog & Leventhal, 2006).

5. Benjamin Filene, *Romancing the Folk: Public Memory and American Roots Music* (Chapel Hill: University of North Carolina Press, 2000); and Neil V. Rosenberg, ed., *Transforming Tradition: Folk Music Revivals Examined* (Urbana: University of Illinois Press, 1993).

SELLING FOLK MUSIC

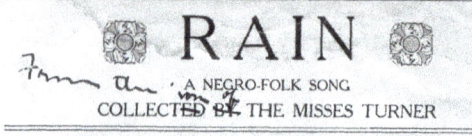

Cecil J. Sharp, ed., *One Hundred English Folksongs* (Philadelphia: Oliver Ditson Co., 1916).

"Rain: A Negro Folk Song Collected by the Misses Turner," sheet music, 1915.

Old Favorite Songs (Lawrenceburg, IN: Lawrenceburg Roller Mills Co., ca. 1915).

Harvey P. Moyer, *Songs of Socialism* (Chicago: Co-Operative Printing Co., 1911).

"The Advancing Proletaire," sheet music, ca. 1915.

Henry Edward Krehbiel, *Afro-American Folksongs: A Study in Racial and National Music* (New York: G. Schirmer, Inc., 1914).

I. W. W. Songs to Fan the Flames of Discontent Joe Hill edition (Cleveland: I. W. W. Publishing Bureau, December 1914).

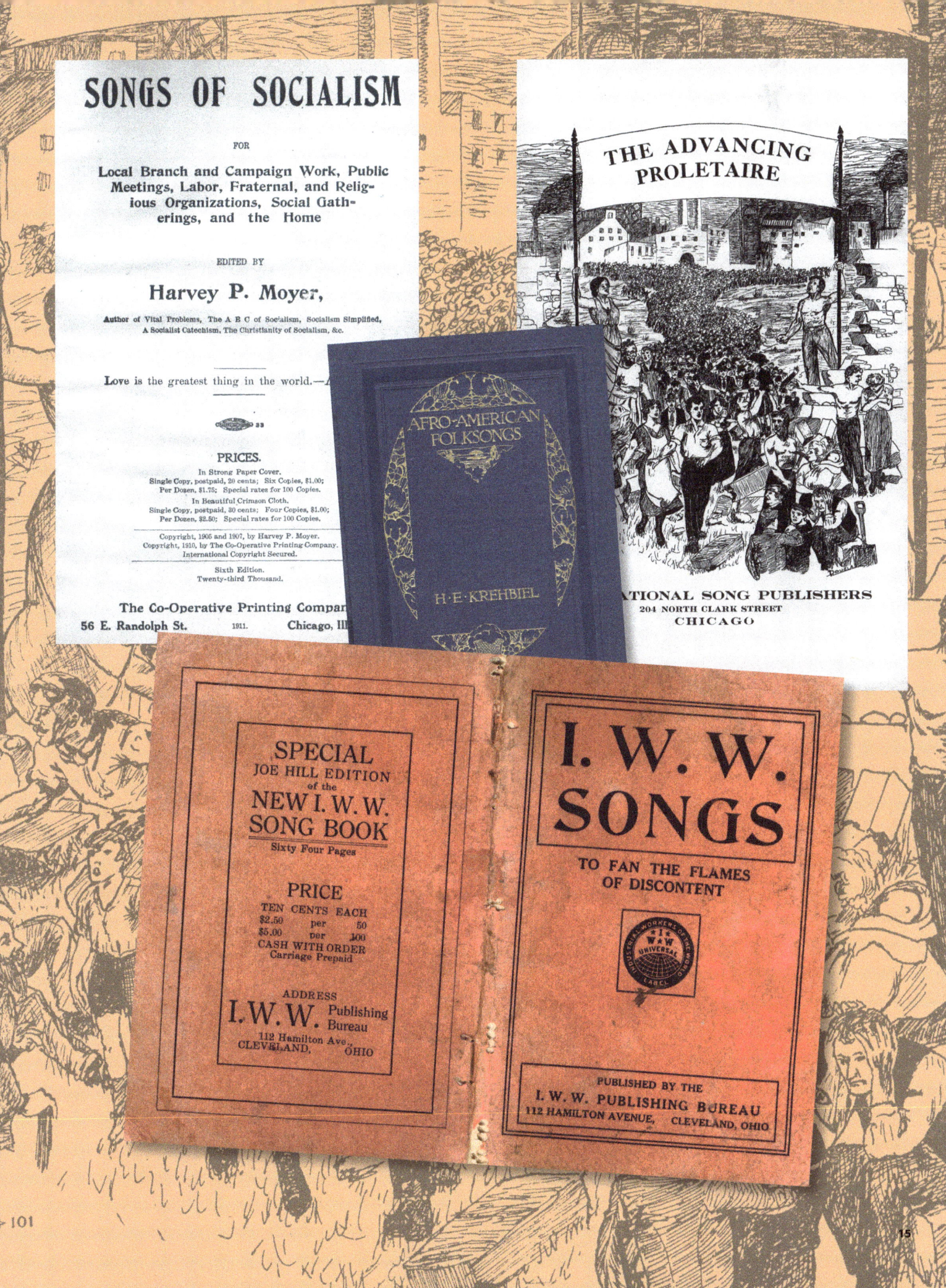

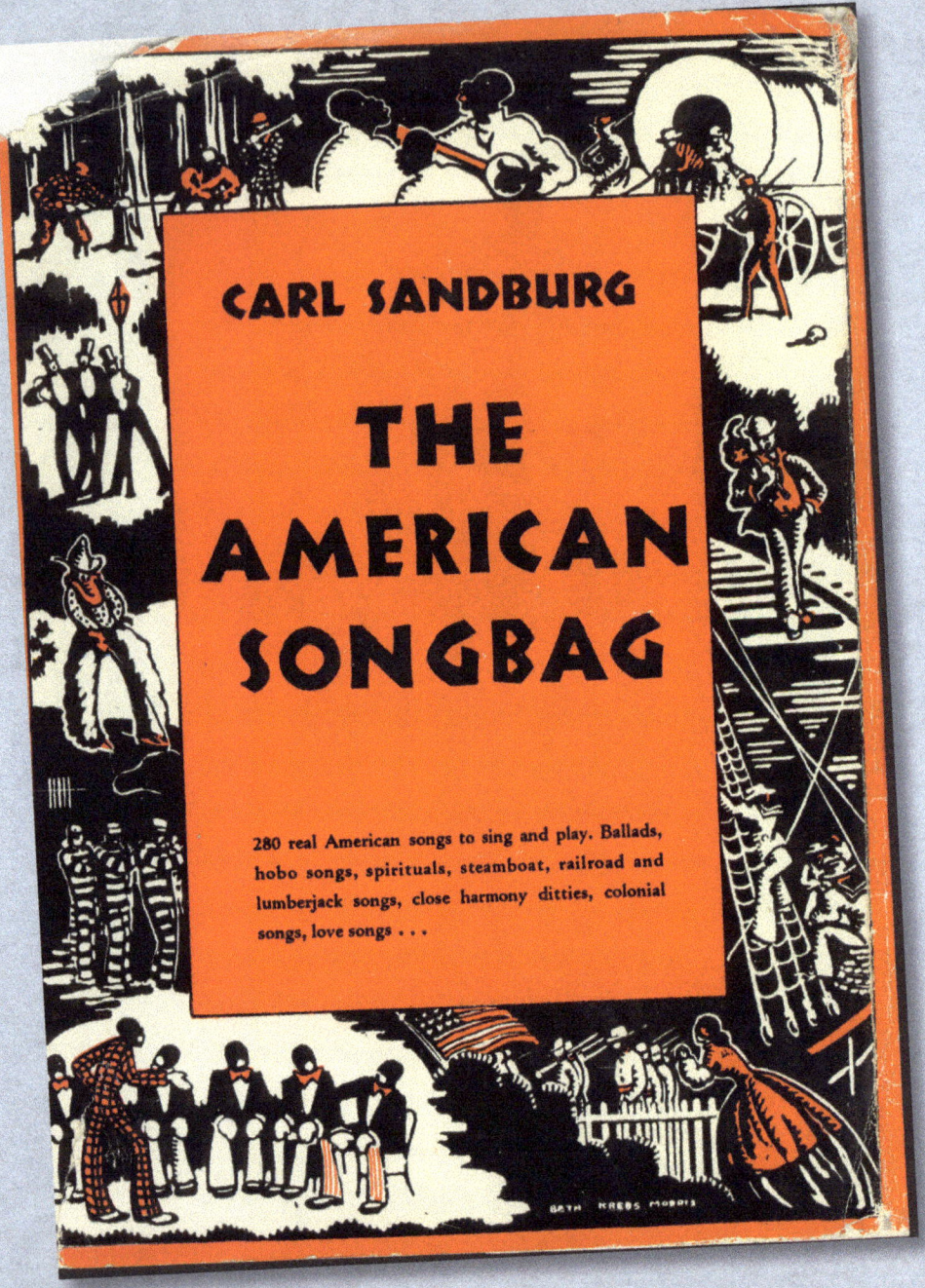

Carl Sandburg, *The American Songbag* (New York: Harcourt, Brace & Co., 1927).

Victor Records, flyer, "Popular Ballads and Mountaineer Tunes," 1927.

Lorraine d'Oremieulx Warner, *A Kindergarten Book of Folk-Songs* (Boston: E. C. Schirmer Music Co., 1922).

Archibald T. Davison and Thomas Whitney Surette, *140 Folk-Songs: Rote Songs for Grades I, II, and III* (Boston: E. C. Schirmer Music Co., 1921).

Bascom Lamar Lunsford and Lamar Stringfield, *30 and 1 Folk Songs from the Southern Mountains* (New York: Carl Fischer, Inc., 1929).

The Hobo in Song and Poetry (Cincinnati: V. C. Anderson, ca. 1920).

Harry "Mac" McClintock, "Halleluiah! I'm a Bum," sheet music (Villa Moret, 1928).

Tom Mix, *Western Songs* (Chicago: M. M. Cole Pub. Co., 1935).

Sixth Annual Berkeley Folk Music Festival, program, June 26–30, 1963.

Gene Autry, *Famous Cowboy Songs and Mountain Ballads* (Chicago: M. M. Cole Pub., 1932).

Tiny Texan, *World's Greatest Collection of Cowboy and Mountain Ballads* (Chicago: M. M. Cole Publishing Co., 1933).

John A. Lomax and Alan Lomax, *Cowboy Songs and Other Frontier Ballads* revised and enlarged edition (New York: Macmillan Co., 1938).

John A. Lomax, *Cowboy Songs* (New York: Sturgis & Walton Co., 1917; original edition, 1910).

Margaret Larkin, *Singing Cowboy: A Book of Western Songs* (New York: Alfred A. Knopf, 1931).

Songs of the Range (Chicago: Belmont Music Co., 1938).

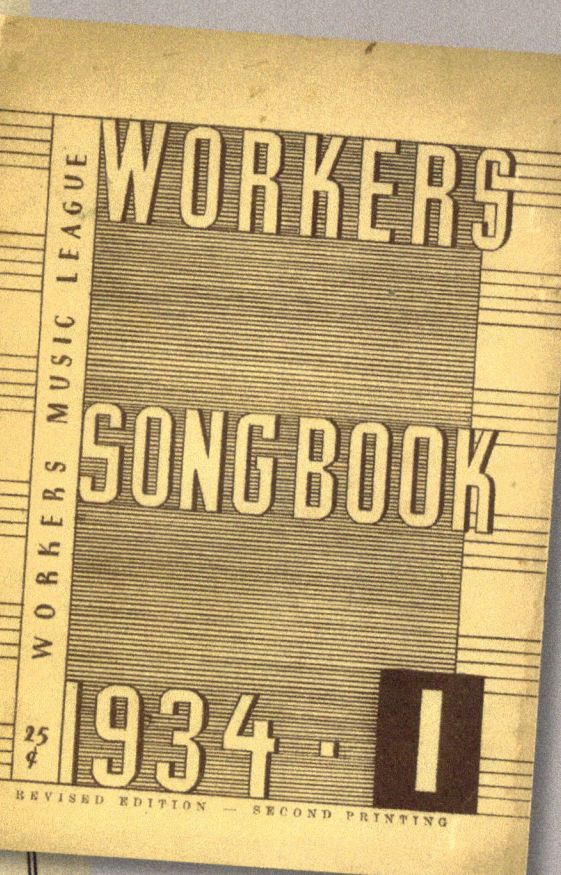

Roy Harris, *Folk-Song Symphony* (G. Schirmer, 1942).

Workers Song Book, No. 1 (New York: Workers Music League, 1934).

Jacob Schaeffer, "Mit Gezang Tzum Kamf" (New York: International Workers Order, 1932), in Yiddish and Hebrew.

"Murderous Minstrel," *Time*, January 14, 1935.

John W. Work, *American Negro Songs and Spirituals* (New York: Bonanza Books, 1940).

MUSIC

Murderous Minstrel

In Texas a black buck known as Lead Belly murdered a man. He sang a petition to Governor Pat Neff and was granted a pardon. Back in the Louisiana swamplands, where he was born Huddie Ledbetter, his knife made more trouble. He was in State Prison at Angola when John A. Lomax, eminent ballad collector, stopped by last summer and asked the warden if he could please hear Lead Belly sing.

John Lomax arrived in Manhattan last week to lecture on ballads and with him was Lead Belly, wild-eyed as ever. The

LEAD BELLY
"Please, Governor Neff, let me go home."

Negro had been pardoned again because Mr. Lomax had made a phonograph record of a second petition and taken it to Louisiana's Governor Allen. Lead Belly was released from prison on Aug. 1. Month later when Mr. Lomax was sitting in a Texas hotel he felt a tap on his shoulder. It was Lead Belly, saying: "Boss, here I is." His knife bulged in his pocket. In his hand was a rickety green-painted guitar held together by string.

Wearing overalls and a blue hickory shirt over a yellow one, Lead Belly sang in Manhattan last week for University of Texas alumni. And John Lomax was nervous. Theatrical agents and radio scouts insisted on hearing his protégé, who had been out on a wild 24-hour rampage in Harlem. Until it was time for him to sing Lomax kept his hell-raising minstrel locked up in a coat room. But the performance went off without mishap. Lead Belly's voice is rich and clear. He plays and sings with his eyes closed, taps single time with one foot, triple with the other. He claims that most of his songs are his own. He sang about when "me and a bunch of cowboys had that famous battle on Bunker Hill," and again about the Negro who "throwed his jelly* out of

the window...
when he cha
him his first
I am your
Please, Go
home.
I know m
When de
steppin'
Please, Go
Have merc
I don't se
If I can't
parole.
Please, G
kind,
And if I
cut my
If I had
got me,
I would w
you free
And I'm
Mary.

Master of

When the
York harbor
ers clambere
brated passe
little man w
ered scarf an
for no appare
& taking off
spectacles pe
he gladly ga
Russian lett
vertically, li
read: "Igor
For the fir
enigmatic of
the sea, whi
U. S., where he knows that even people
who fail to understand his music will pay
to see him. In Manhattan he was given his
first reception by the League of Composers, long hospitable to all his efforts. Before he returns to Eur
Stravinsky will have condu
tras in Milwaukee, Chicago
Angeles, Boston. Other
him as a pianist when he
tions of his works with
Dushkin.*

By way of the piano St
a composer more impo
pions insist, than Richar
Sibelius, the other grea
tury music. Stravinsky
at the Maryinsky The
encouraged the boy s
content to remain an
dutifully to the Unive
but his marks were co
20 the die of his ca
the great Rimsky-Ko
a pupil.

Under Rimsky, S
first dazzling orches
the late Sergei Diag
the young composer
Diaghilev and his

*Stravinsky-Dushki
for Minneapolis, Ch
Indianapolis, San Fr
Los Angeles, Montre

---
*A "jelly" in the Louisiana swamplands means a very fat woman. Many of Lead Belly's songs are in Lomax's excellent book, *American Ballads and Folk Songs* (Macmillan, $5).

LEAD BELLY
"Please, Governor Neff, let me go home."

(advertisement left side)

less...

...acture a product that ...r can harm—take care. ...weather can "break" a ...or materials and factory ...are sensitive to atmos-...

...perate an *un-air-conditioned* ...tre, hotel, retail store, a-...r office building... be ...dark cloud looms on your ...orizon. It won't be long ...ur patrons may refuse to ...r palm with silver unless ...your business climate.

...than 30 years Parks engi-...ve been correcting sales and ...on troubles by substituting ...d Climate for *uncontrolled* cli-...ertified Climate supplies clean ...the right temperature and hu-.... It improves products, aids ...sses and increases human com-...nd effectiveness.

...nsultation with Parks engineers ... nothing. Write us... or send ...he folder—"A Guide For Those ...o Must Outwit Climate."

PARKS
Certified CLIMATE

PARKS-CRAMER COMPANY
FITCHBURG, MASSACHUSETTS

"The Immortal Negro Melodies: These are Songs Paul Robeson Sings," supplement to the *Family Journal*, November 6, 1937 (published in England).

"John Henry," program with Paul Robeson and Josh White, December 25, 1939.

"White Top Folk Festival," flyer, Virginia, August 12–13, 1938.

John A. Lomax and Alan Lomax, *Negro Folk Songs as Sung by Lead Belly* (New York: Macmillan Co., 1936).

NEGRO FOLK SONGS
AS SUNG BY LEAD BELLY

Photograph by Otto Hesse

JOHN A. LOMAX • ALAN LOMAX

Lawrence Gellert, *Negro Songs of Protest* (New York: American Music League, 1936).

Notice of Carter Family Concert, 1935.

John A. Lomax and Alan Lomax, *American Ballads & Folk Songs* (New York: Macmillan Co., 1934).

Three Cowboy Desperado Songs (New York: Carl Fischer, 1928).

Melvin LeMon, *The Miner Sings* (New York: J. Fischer & Bro., 1936).

Play and Sing: America's Greatest Collection of Old Time Songs and Mountain Ballads! (Chicago: M. M. Cole Pub., 1930).

Big Bill Campbell, "The Hill-Billy 'Round-Up' Songbook," published in the *Wild West Weekly*, March 12, 1938, in England.

Mountain Songs (Chicago: Belmont Music Co., 1937).

"The Kentucky Wonder Bean": Walter Peterson (Chicago: M. M. Cole Pub. Co., 1931).

Treasure Chest of Homespun Songs (New York: Treasure Chest Publications, 1935).

John Jacob Niles, *More Songs of the Hill-Folk* (New York: G. Schirmer, 1936).

John Jacob Niles, *Songs of the Hill-Folk* (New York: G. Schirmer, 1934).

Samuel H. Friedman, *Rebel Song Book* (New York: Rand School Press, 1935).

Zilphia Horton, *Labor Songs* (New York: Textile Workers Union of America, 1939).

Songs of the People (New York: Workers Library Publishers, 1937).

Red Song Book (New York: Workers Library Publishers, 1932).

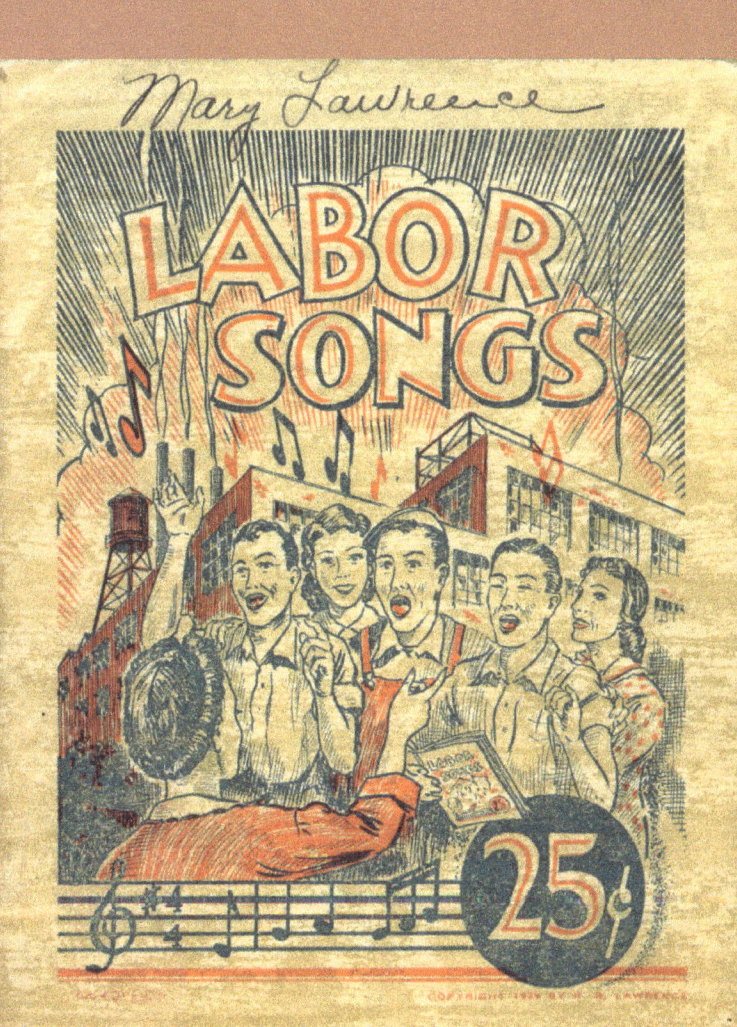
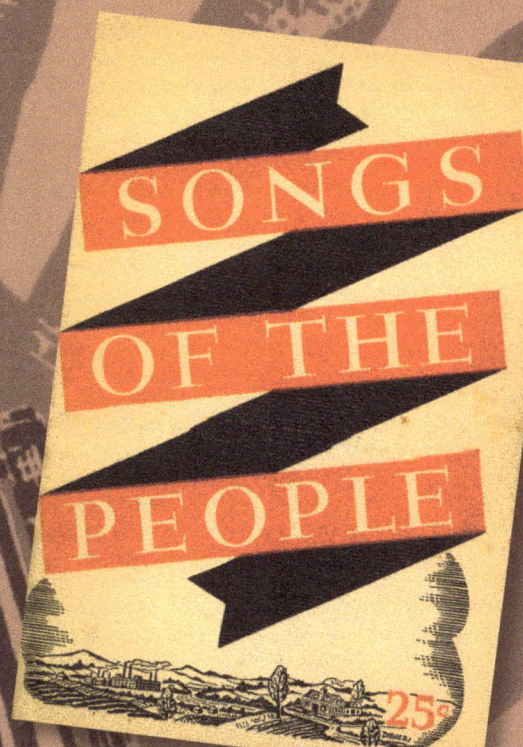

Songs of the Plains (Chicago: Belmont Music Co., 1938).

Popular Cowboy Songs (New York: Hobo News, ca. 1935).

Cowboy Songs (Chicago: Belmont Music Co., 1937).

Cowboy Songs as Sung by John White (Hollywood: Gordon Music Co., 1934).

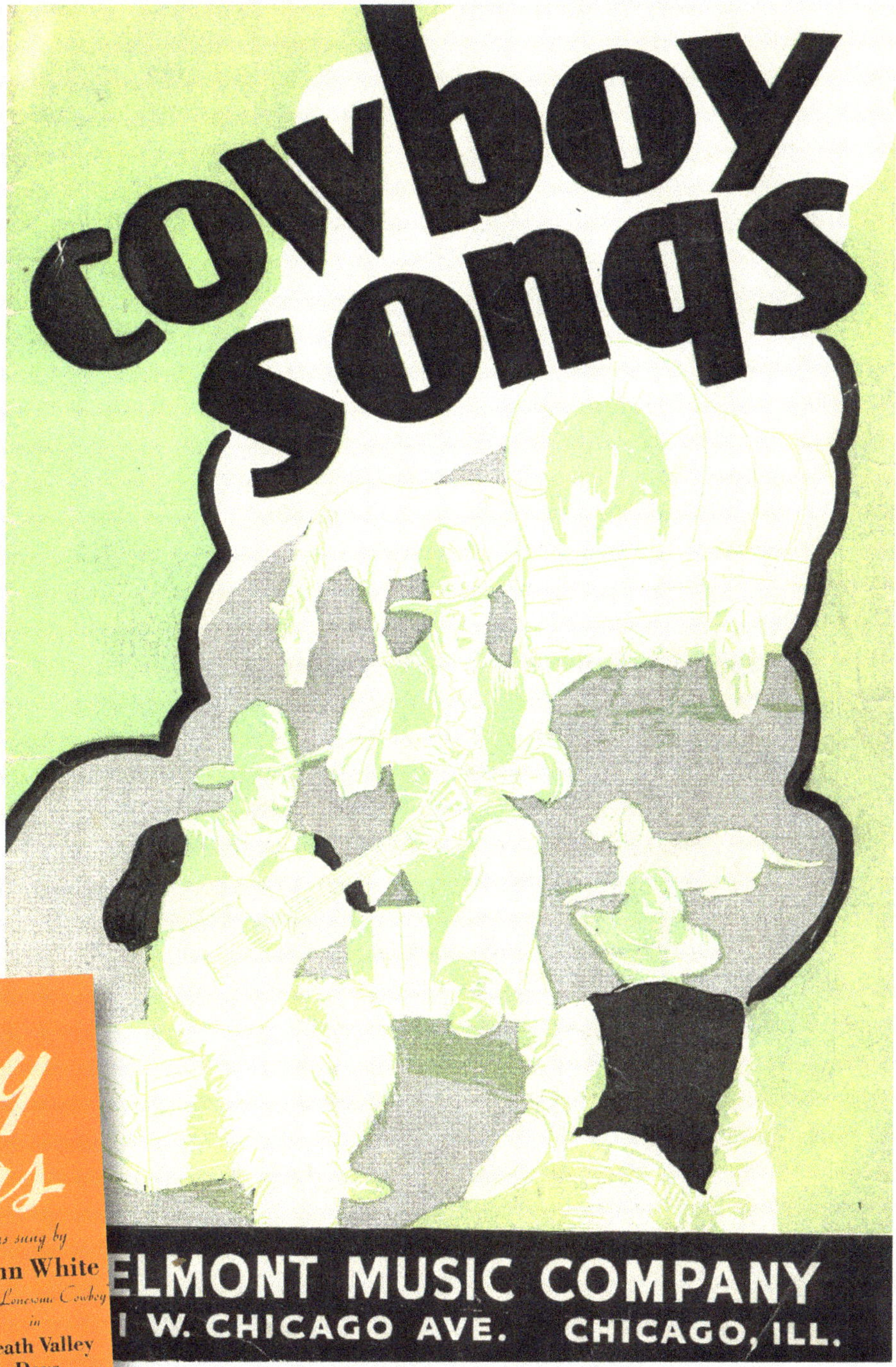
Cowboy
Songs
ELMONT MUSIC COMPANY
I W. CHICAGO AVE. CHICAGO, ILL.

Cowboy
Songs
as sung by
John White
"The Lonesome Cowboy"
in
Death Valley
Days
Compliments of
PACIFIC COAST BORAX CO.
New York

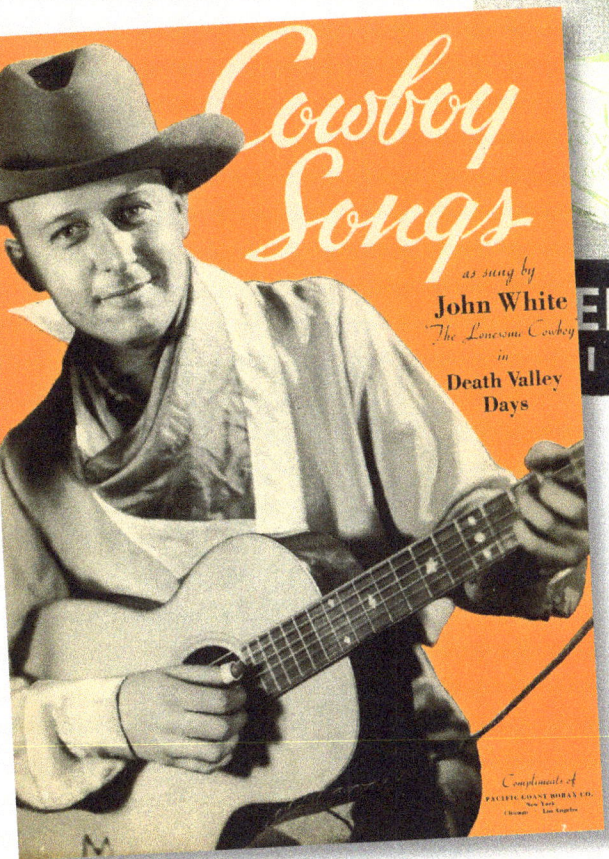

Lead Belly and the Golden Gate Quartet, *"The Midnight Special" and Other Southern Prison Songs* (Victor, P-50, 1940).

Josh White, *Strange Fruit* (Keynote Recordings, 125, 1944).

Lead Belly, *Negro Sinful Songs* (Musicraft, 31, 1939).

Lead Belly, Woody Guthrie, and Cisco Houston, *Midnight Special* (Disc Company of America, 726, 1947).

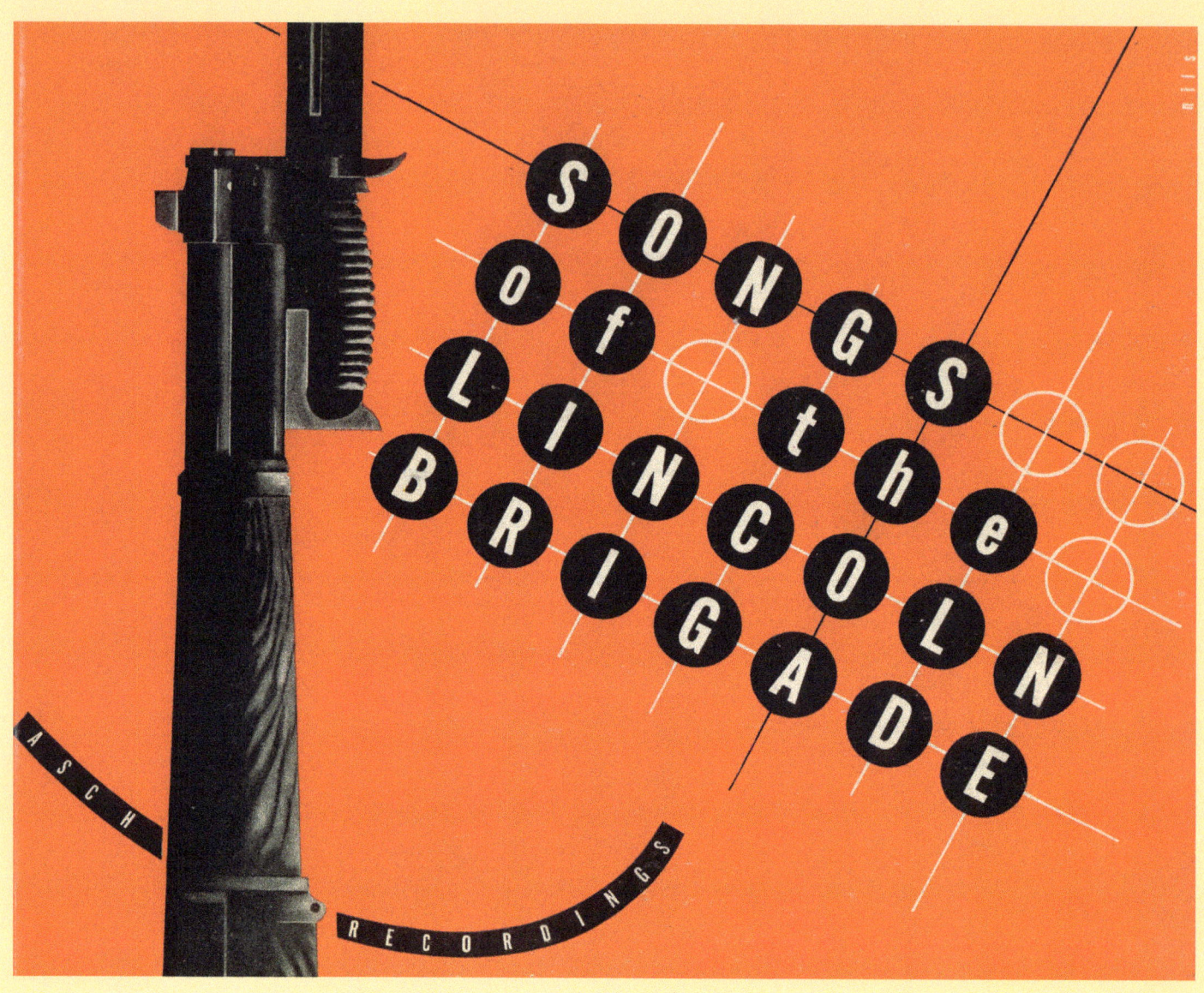

Songs of the Lincoln Brigade (Asch Recordings, A330, 1943).

Josh White, promo advertisement, February 1946.

WWVA World's Original Radio Jamboree Famous Songs (Chicago: M. M. Cole Pub. Co., 1942).

Woody Guthrie, *American Folksong* (New York: Disc Company of America, 1947).

Doc Hopkins and His Country Boys (Chicago: M. M. Cole Pub. Co., 1945).

Boone County Jamboree: Favorite Songs of the WLW (Chicago: M. M. Cole Pub., Co., 1941).

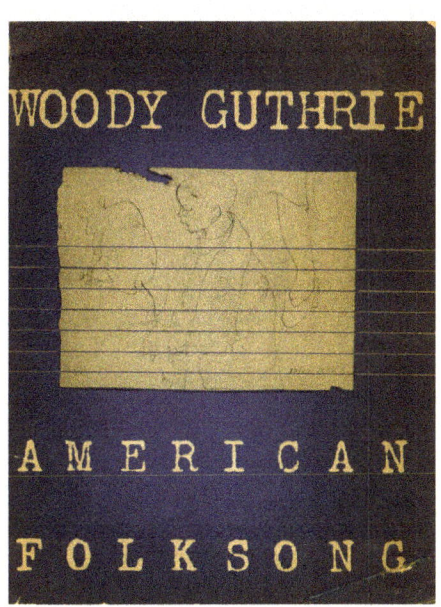

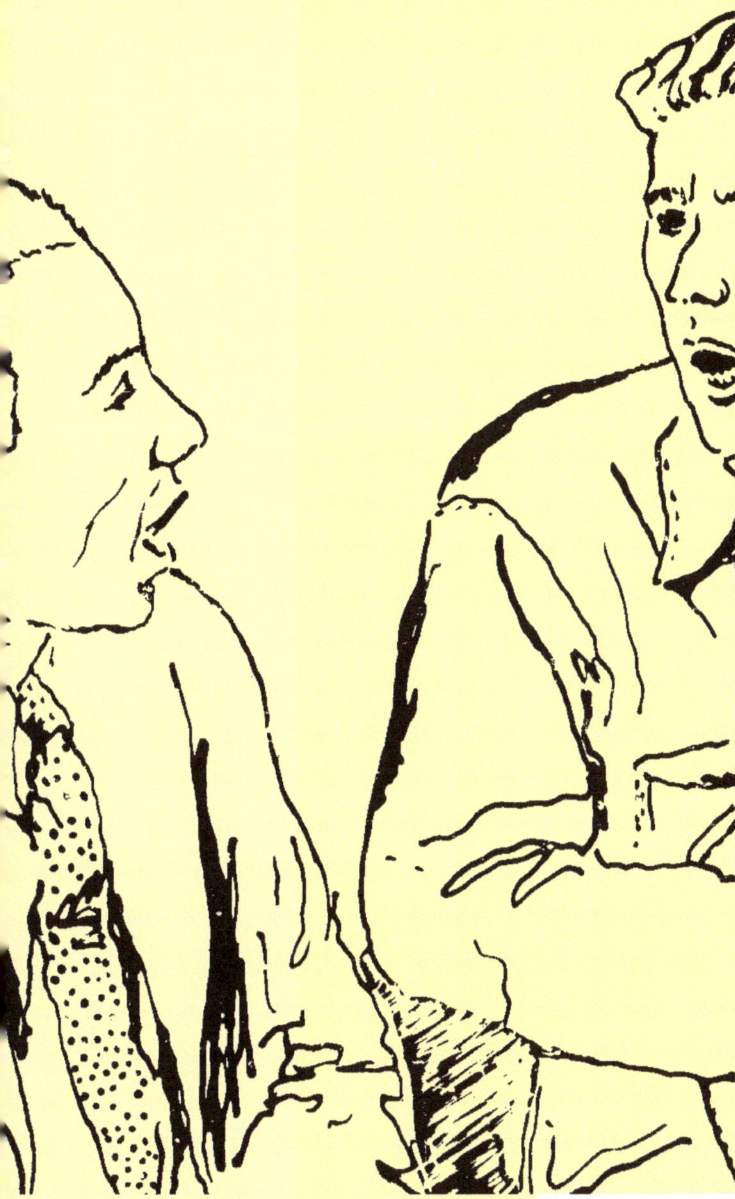

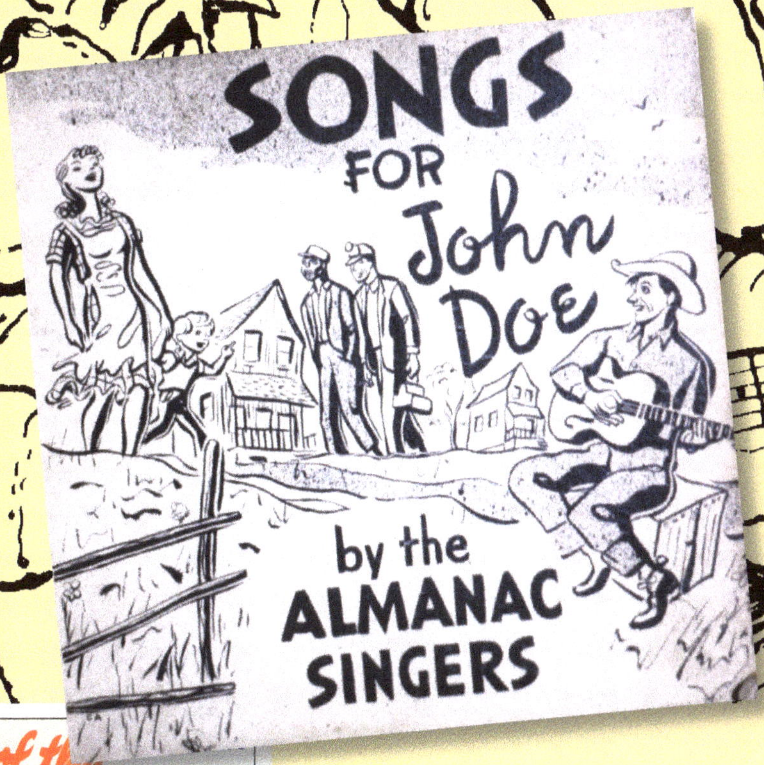

EARLY ALMANAC SINGERS SONGBOOK.

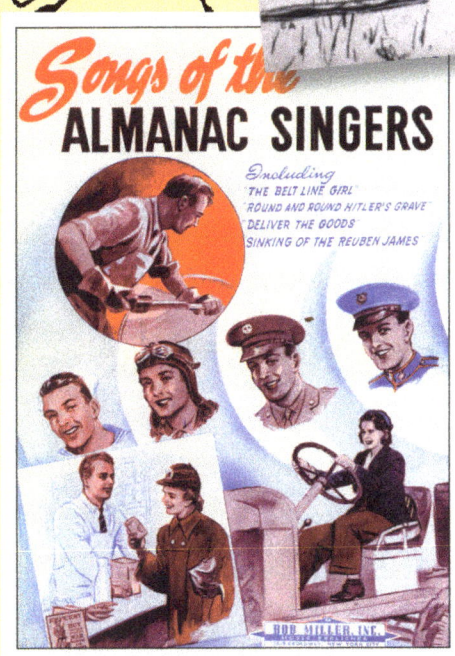

Lonesome Valley: A Collection of American Folk Music (Folkways Records, FA, 2010, 1950, but recorded 1943–1946).

Woody Guthrie, *Bound for Glory* (New York: E. P. Dutton & Co., 1943).

Almanac Singers, *Songs for John Doe* (Almanac Records, 102, 1941).

Songs of the Almanac Singers (New York: Bob Miller, 1942).

DELMORE BROTHERS (Alton and Rabon)
(Singing with violin and guitars)
B-8687 That Yodelin' Gal, Miss Julie
Take Me Back to the Range

CLAUDE CASEY and his Pine State Playboys
(Singing with string band)
B-8697 What's Wrong with Me Now?
It Doesn't Matter

MONTANA SLIM (The Yodeling Cowboy)
(With guitar)
B-8696 I Bought a Rock for a Rocky Mountain Gal
Streamlined Yodel Song

ROY HALL and his Blue Ridge Entertainers
(String band with singing)
B-8702 She's Winkin' at Me
Your Heart Should Belong to Me

LYRIC QUARTET (Male quartet with piano)
B-8698 I Can Tell You the Time
Somebody Loves Me

The JONES BROTHERS TRIO
(Singing with accordion)
B-8707 The Cross on the Hill
My Soul Will Shout Hallelujah

BYRON PARKER and his Mountaineers
(Singing and Fiddling with string band)
B-8708 Tell Her Not to Wait For Me
Married Life Blues

BLUE SKY BOYS (Bill and Earl Bolick)
(Singing with mandolin and guitar)
B-8693 In the Hills of Roane County
Brown Eyes

ARTHUR SMITH and his Dixie Liners
(Singing and Fiddling with string band)
B-8688 That's the Love I Have for You
Peacock Rag

CHARLES MITCHELL and his Orchestra
B-8716 Jersey Side Jive—F.T.
The Sun Has Gone Down on Our Love
—F.T. (V.R.)

The VILLAGE BOYS
B-8717 A Paul Jones Dance
I'm Doin' a Peach of a Job—F.T. (V.R.)
(With a Little Peach Down in Ga.)

BILL MOUNCE and Sons of the South
B-8718 Adios—Polka
Kickin' It Off—F.T. (V.R.)

JIMMY HART and his Merrymakers
B-8719 Cheatin' on Me—F.T. (V.R.)
It's Kinda Late to Be Sorry—F.T. (V.R.)

NETTLE BROTHERS String Band
(Bill and Norman Nettles)
B-8720 Fannin' Street Blues—(V.R.)
Dan, the Banana Man—(V.R.)

BILL BOYD and his Cowboy Ramblers
B-8721 Swing Steel, Swing—F.T.
I'll Be Back in a Year, Little Darlin'
—F.T. (V.R.)

NEW RACE RECORDS

TOMMY McCLENNAN
(Blues singer with guitar)
B-8689 Katy Mae Blues
Love With a Feeling
B-8704 Black Minnie
Drop Down Mama

The FOUR CLEFS
B-8690 Returning—F.T. (V.R.)
You'll Always Dwell in My Heart—F.T. (V.R.)

HEAVENLY GOSPEL SINGERS
(Male quartet unaccompanied)
B-8695 The Lord God Is My Shepherd
Walk Together Chillun

WALTER DAVIS
(Blues singer with piano)
B-8694 I Hate to Say Goodbye
Soon Forgotten

WASHBOARD SAM and his Washboard Band
B-8699 Just to Prove I Love You—Slow Blues
Come On Back—F.T.

HUDDIE LEADBELLY
(Blues singer with guitar)
B-8709 Roberta
The Red Cross Store Blues

CLARA MORRIS
(Blues singer with piano and guitar)
B-8700 I'm Blue, Daddy
I Stagger in My Sleep

The CATS and the FIDDLE
B-8705 Crawlin' Blues—F.T. (V.R.)
Until I Met You—Slow F.T. (V.R.)

The FIVE BREEZES
(Blues singing with guitar)
B-8710 Laundry Man
Just a Jitterbug

ALPHABETICAL LIST OF OLD FAMILIAR and RACE RECORDS FOR JUNE AND JULY, 1941

For Records listed previously, please refer to the June, 1941 Bluebird Old Familiar Tunes and Race Catalog—at your Bluebird Record Dealer's.

B-8718 Adios—Polka............Bill Mounce & Sons of the South
B-8686 Birmingham Woman............Texas Jim Robertson
B-8704 Black Minnie............Tommy McClennan

35¢ BLUEBIRD
Made by RCA Victor
OLD FAMILIAR TUNES and RACE RECORDS
JULY, 1941
Leading Artists .. Finer Recordings .. Better Material
RCA VICTOR DIVISION, RCA MANUFACTURING COMPANY, INC., CAMDEN, N.J.

OLD FAMILIAR TUNES—NEW RECORDS

TEXAS JIM ROBERTSON
(Singing with violin, accordion and guitar)
B-8686 Brother Henry
Birmingham Woman
B-8706 There's a Heart In the Heart of the Rockies
Too Blue to Cry

BILL MONROE and his Blue Grass Boys
(Singing with string band)
B-8692 Dog House Blues
Katy Hill

ELTON BRITT
(Singing with guitar, violin and accordion)
B-8701 There's So Much That I Forgot
I'll Die Before I Tell You

The HAPPY VALLEY BOYS
(Singing with guitars)
B-8703 You Don't Love Me
Weeping Willow Valley

JOHNNY BARFIELD
(Singing with violin and guitar)
B-8691 True to the One I Love
Pretty Little Napanee

Old Familiar Tunes and Race Records, RCA Victor Bluebird catalog, 1941.

Booklet for *The Songs of Early America* (Bost Records, ES1, 1942).

Catalog of Stinson Asch Records.

Booklet for *Sing Out, Sweet Land* (Decca Records, 1946).

Booklet for Burl Ives, *The Wayfaring Stranger* (Asch 345, 1944).

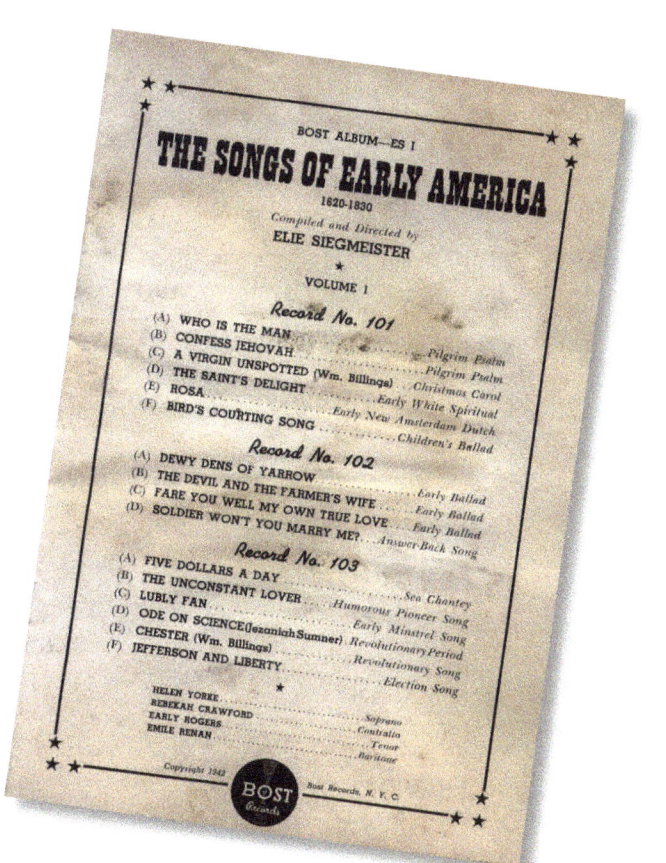

"On Top of Old Smoky," sheet music, 1944.

Jack Guthrie and Woody Guthrie, "Oklahoma Hills," sheet music, 1945.

Burl Ives, "The Blue Tail Fly," sheet music, 1945.

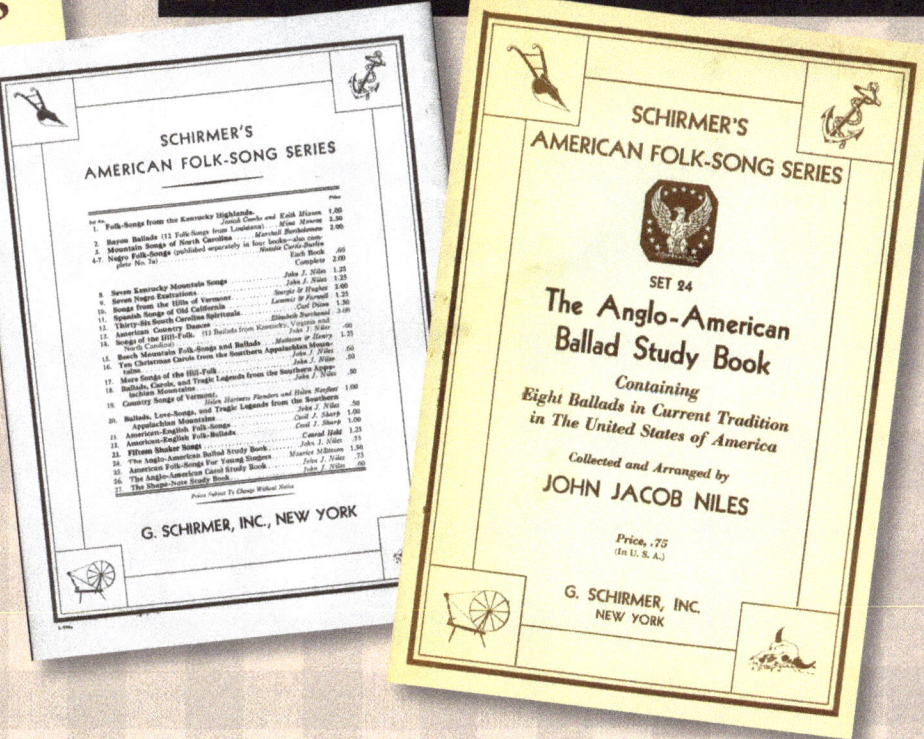

Lewis Allan and Earl Robinson, "The House I Live In," sheet music, 1942.

Hy Zaret and Lou Singer, "One Meat Ball," sheet music, 1944.

John Jacob Niles, "Go 'Way from My Window," sheet music, 1944.

Schirmer's American Folk-Song Series, flyer (New York: G. Schirmer).

John Jacob Niles, *The Anglo-American Ballad Study Book* (New York: G. Schirmer, Inc., 1945).

Elie Siegmeister, *Work and Sing* (New York: William R. Scott, Inc., 1944).

10 New Songs the Soviets Sing, English lyrics by Harold J. Rome (New York: Am-Rus Music Corporation, 1943).

Josef Marais, *Songs from the Veld* (New York: G. Schirmer, 1942).

Ad for Almanac Singers, *Songs for John Doe*, *New Masses*, May 20, 1941.

Richard Dyer-Bennet concert, flyer, Town Hall, New York City, January 31, 1948.

Flyers for People's Songs Hootenanny with Pete Seeger, Betty Sanders, and Bernie Asbel, Cleveland, February 9, 1947.

Josh White concert, program, Orchestra Hall, Chicago, January 31, 1948.

Concert notices for American People's Festival and Testimonial to Rockwell Kent, *New Masses*, May 20, 1941.

Paul Robeson, program, May 10, 1942, benefit for Highlander Folk School, with Lead Belly, Sonny Terry and Brownie McGhee.

Paul Robeson concert, flyer, Fresno Memorial Auditorium, February 28, 1946.

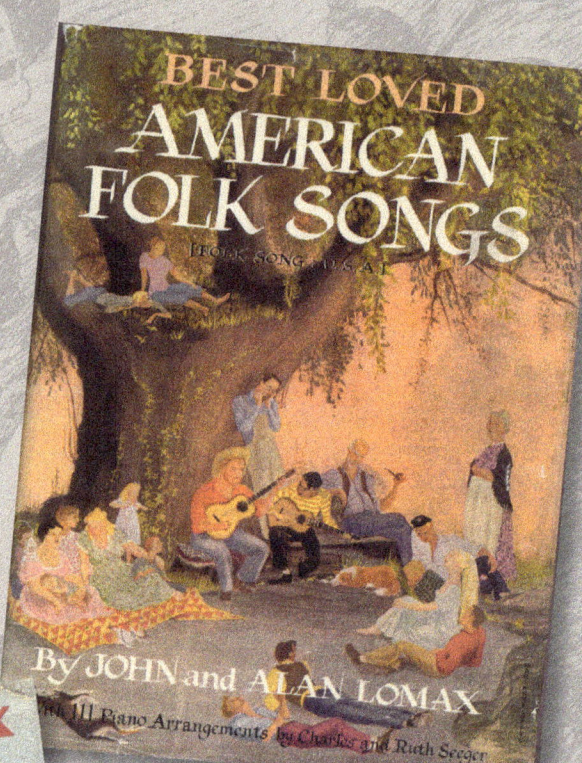
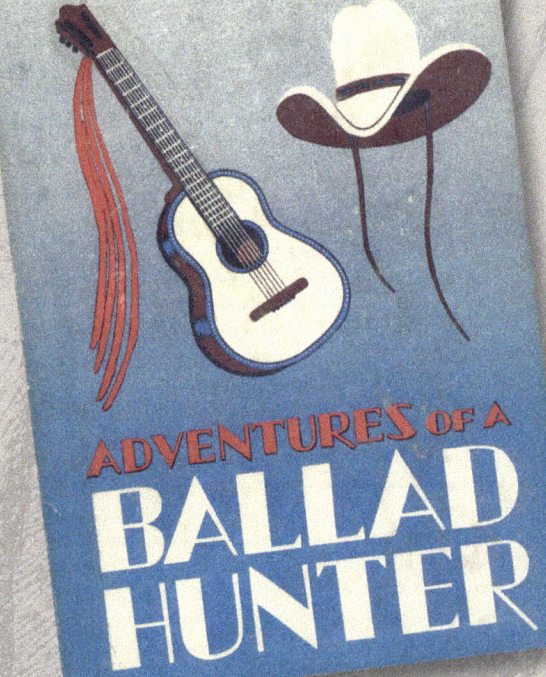

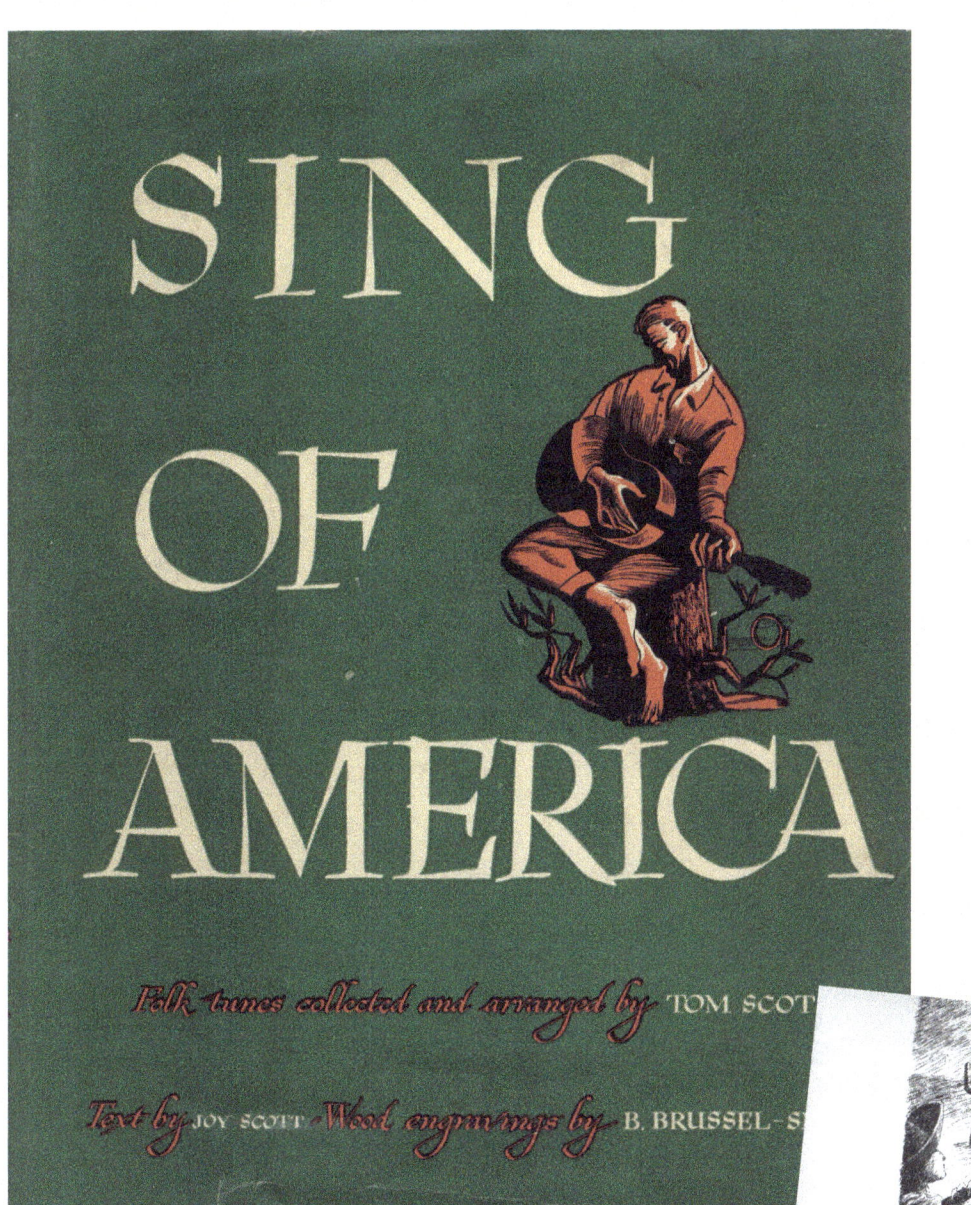

Burl Ives, *Wayfaring Stranger* (New York: Whittlesey House, 1948).

John A. Lomax and Alan Lomax, *Best Loved American Folk Songs* (New York: Grosset & Dunlap, 1947).

John A. Lomax, *Adventures of a Ballad Hunter* (New York: Macmillan Co., 1947).

Tom Scott, *Sing of America* (New York: Thomas Y. Crowell Co., 1947).

14 Traditional Spanish Songs from Texas (Washington, DC: Music Division, Pan American Union, 1942, from recordings made in Texas, 1934–1939, by John A., Ruby T., and Alan Lomax).

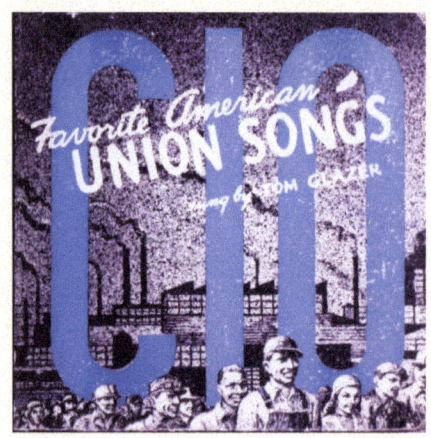

Tom Glazer, *Favorite American Union Songs* (CIO Department of Education and Research, 1950).

Roll the Union On (Asch Recordings, 370, 1946).

Almanac Singers, *Talking Union* (Keynote Recordings, 106, 1941).

Songs of Citizen CIO (Asch, 349, 1944).

Manhattan Chorus, "On the Picket Line" (Timely Records, 1938).

Jefferson Chorus, "Solidarity Forever" and "Union Maid" (Union Records, U-304, 1946).

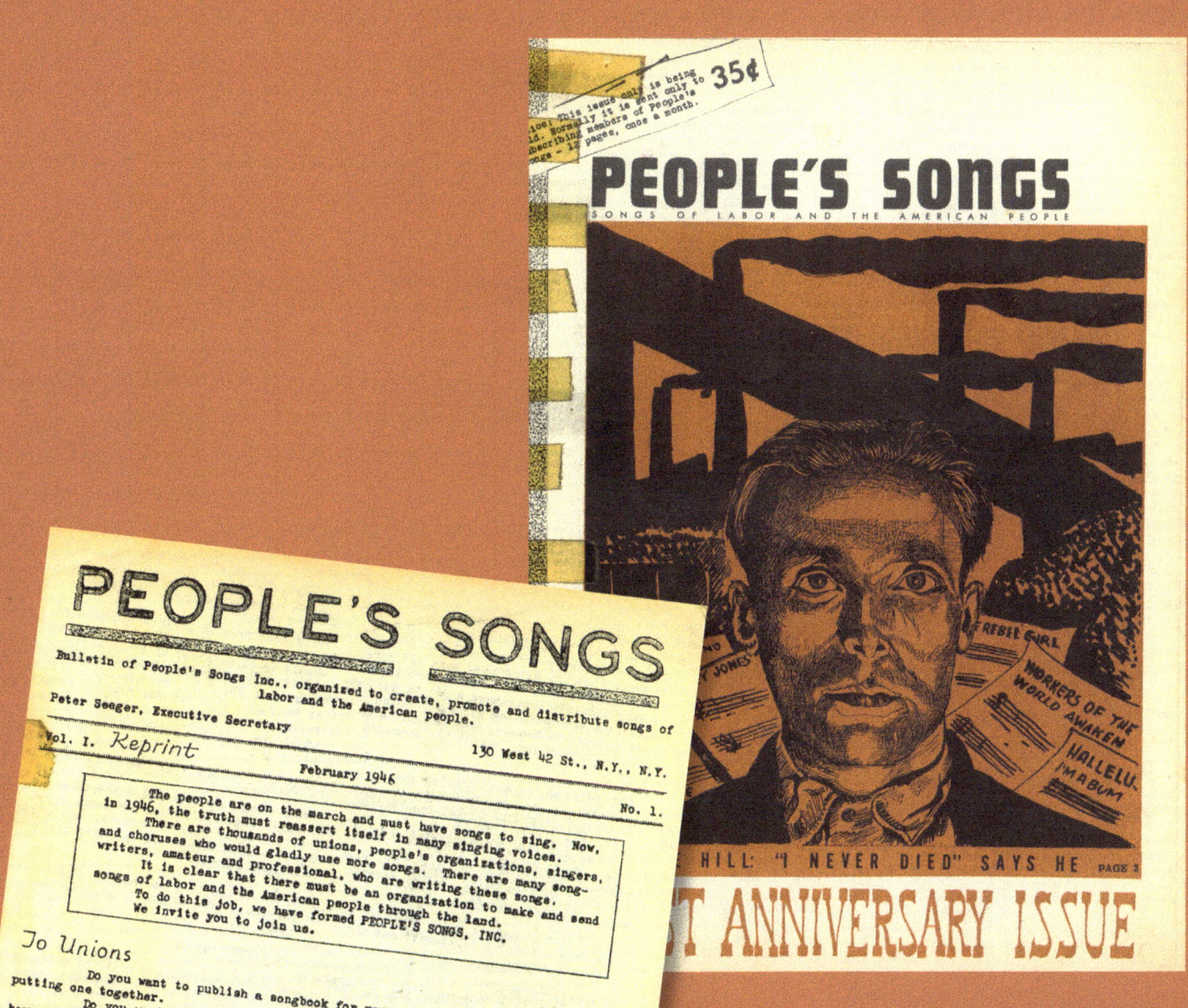

People's Songs, vol. 1, no. 1, February 1946.

People's Songs, vol. 2, nos. 1 and 2, February and March 1947.

Matchbook, "3 Great Philco Radio Shows: Bing Crosby, Don McNeill, Burl Ives," 1946.

Wallace campaign records: "Round the Same Merry Go Round" (Bill Wolfe and Ray Glazer), 1948.

Wallace campaign records: "I've Got a Ballot" (E. Y. Harburg and Alan Lomax), 1948.

Tom Glazer, "Libby's Tomato Juice Song" (David Kurlan Productions), ca. late 1940s.

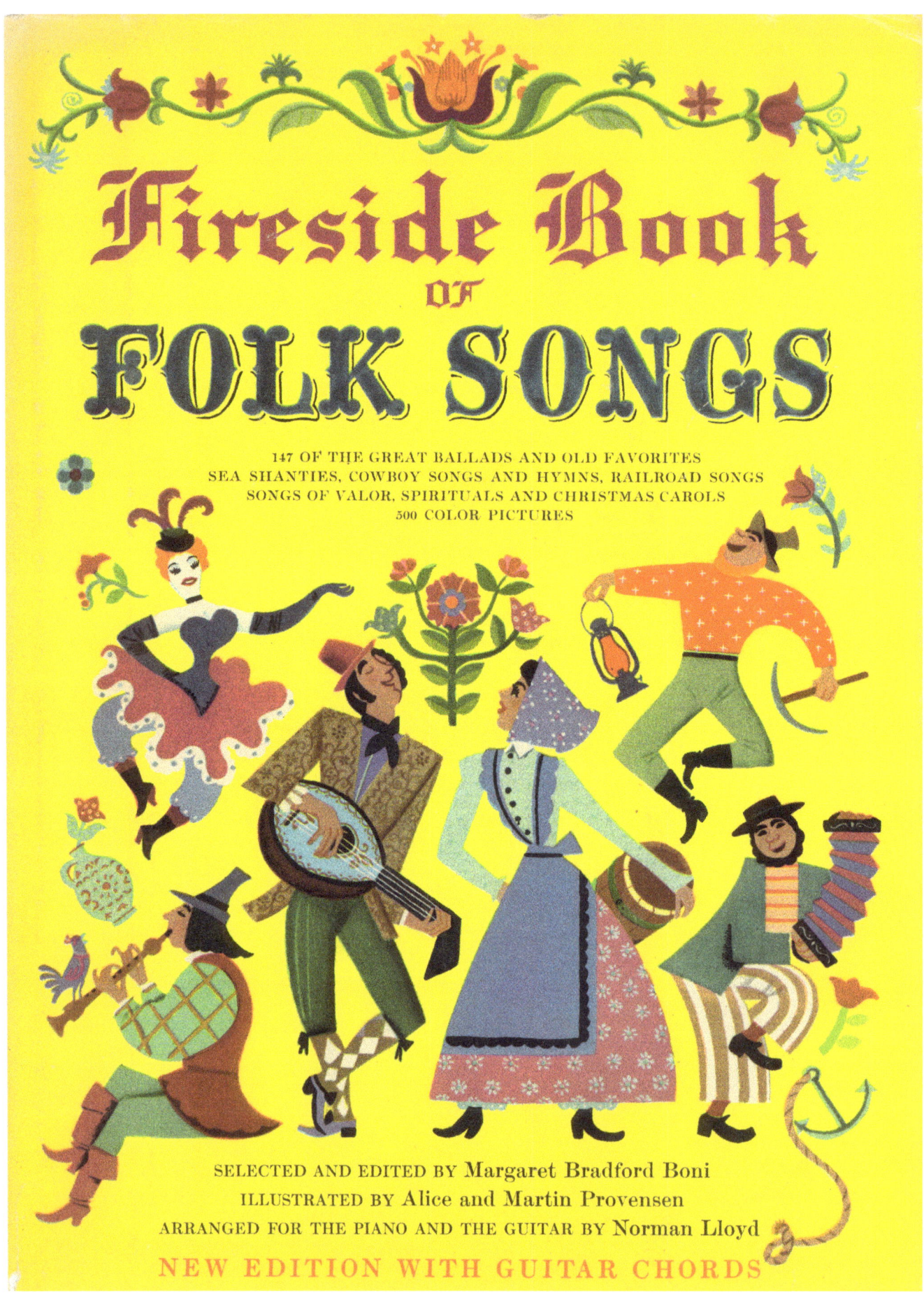

Margaret Boni, *Fireside Book of Folk Songs* (New York: Simon and Schuster, 1947).

Burl Ives, *The Wayfarin' Stranger* songbook (New York: Leeds Music Corp., 1945).

Beatrice Landeck, *Git On Board: Folk Songs for Group Singing* (New York: Edward B. Marks Music Corp., 1944).

Richard Dyer-Bennet, *The 20th Century Minstrel* (New York: Leeds Music Corp., 1946).

Horace Grenell, ed., *The Young People's Records Folk Song Book* (New York: Young People's Records, Inc., 1949; revised edition, Greystone Corp., ca. 1952).

Ruth Crawford Seeger, *American Folk Songs for Children* (New York: Doubleday & Co., 1948).

Beatrice Landeck, *Songs to Grow On* (New York: Edward B. Marks Corp., 1950).

Beatrice Landeck, *More Songs to Grow On* (New York: Edward B. Marks Corp., 1954).

Frank Sinatra, "Goodnight, Irene," sheet music, 1950.

Wally Wicken, "Goodnight, Irene," Canadian sheet music, 1950.

The Weavers, "Goodnight, Irene," sheet music, 1950.

Harry Smith, booklet for *Anthology of American Folk Music* (Folkways FP 251–FP 253, 1952).

Sing Out! vol. 9, no. 1, Summer 1959.

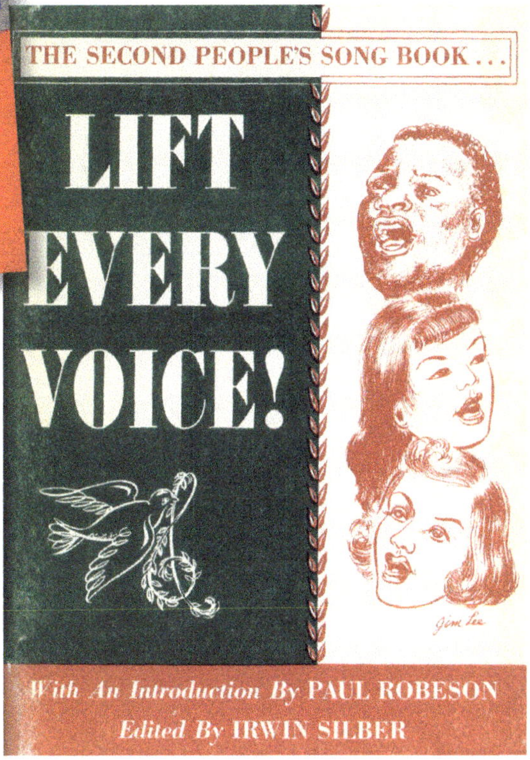

Terry Gilkyson, Frank Miller, and Richard Dehr, "Marianne," sheet music, 1955.

Bob Barron [aka Bob Nemiroff] and Burt Long [aka Burt D'Lugoff], "Cindy, Oh Cindy," sheet music, 1956.

Oscar Brand, "A Guy Is a Guy," sheet music, 1952.

Josef Marais, "A-Round the Corner," sheet music, 1950.

Tom Glazer, "Old Soldiers Never Die," sheet music, 1951.

Don Cherry, "So Long, It's Been Good to Know Yuh," sheet music, 1950. Sing Out! vol. 2, no. 1, July 1951.

The Weavers on cover of *The Cash Box*, August 12, 1950.

Sing Out! vol. 2, no. 1, July 1951.

Sing Out! vol. 4, no. 1, December 1953.

Waldemar Hille, *The People's Song Book* (New York: Boni and Gaer, 1948).

Irwin Silber, *Lift Every Voice! The Second People's Song Book* (New York: People's Artists, 1953).

The Weavers, "When the Saints Go Marching In," sheet music, 1951.

The Weavers, "So Long, It's Been Good to Know Yuh," sheet music, 1950.

The Weavers, "Tzena Tzena Tzena," sheet music, 1950.

The Weavers, "The Roving Kind," sheet music, 1950.

The Weavers, "Wimoweh," sheet music, 1951.

The Weavers, "Taking It Easy," sheet music, 1953.

The Kingston Trio, "The M.T.A.," sheet music, 1956.

The Weavers, "Tom Dooley," sheet music, 1958.

The Kingston Trio, "A Worried Man," sheet music, 1959.

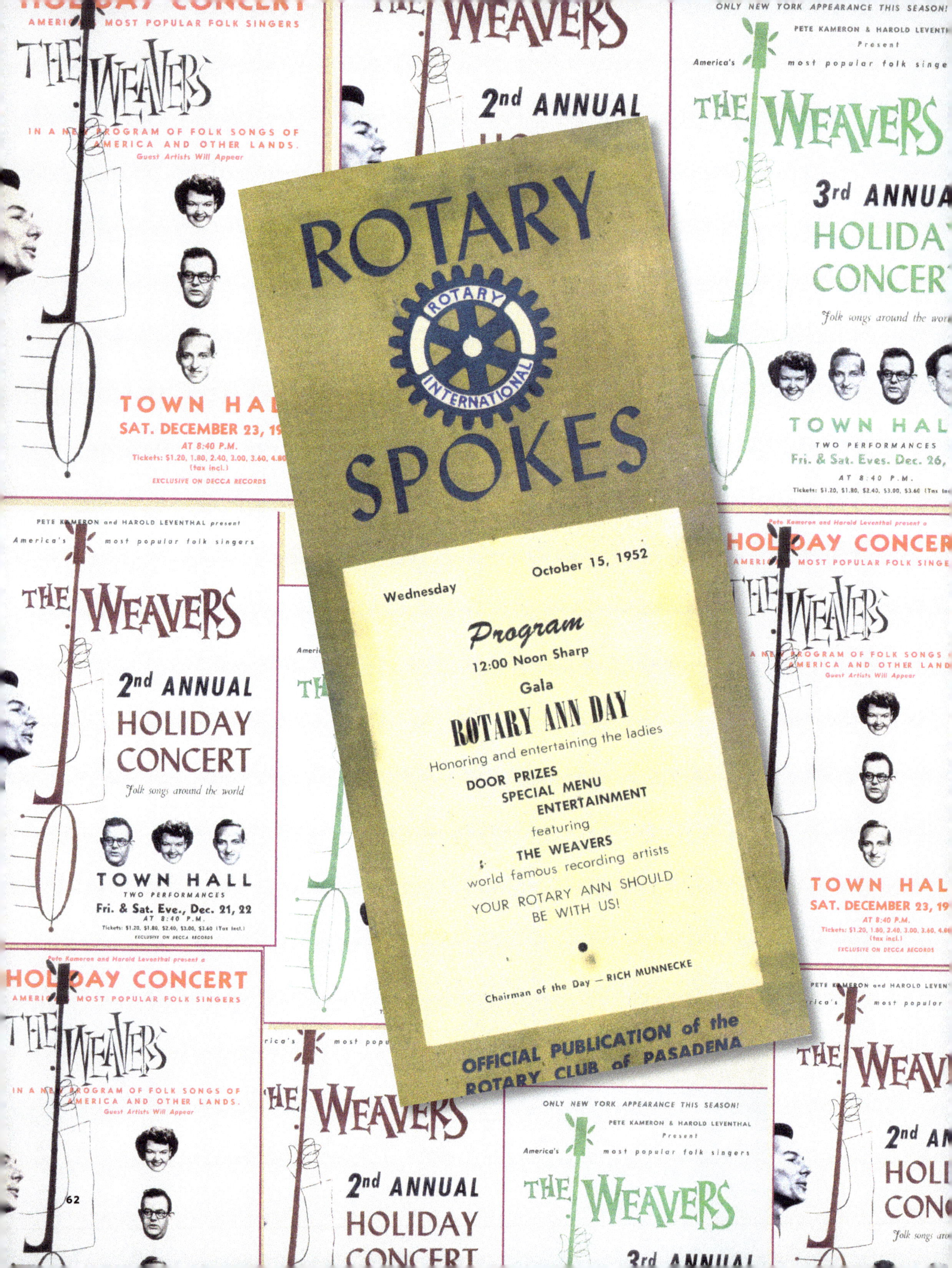
ROTARY
ROTARY INTERNATIONAL
SPOKES
Wednesday
October 15, 1952
Program
12:00 Noon Sharp
Gala
ROTARY ANN DAY
Honoring and entertaining the ladies
DOOR PRIZES
SPECIAL MENU
ENTERTAINMENT
featuring
THE WEAVERS
world famous recording artists
YOUR ROTARY ANN SHOULD
BE WITH US!
Chairman of the Day — RICH MUNNECKE
OFFICIAL PUBLICATION of the
ROTARY CLUB of PASADENA
Pete Kameron and Harold Leventhal present a
HOLIDAY CONCERT
AMERICA'S MOST POPULAR FOLK SINGERS
THE WEAVERS
IN A NEW PROGRAM OF FOLK SONGS OF AMERICA AND OTHER LANDS.
Guest Artists Will Appear
TOWN HALL
SAT. DECEMBER 23, 19
AT 8:40 P.M.
Tickets: $1.20, 1.80, 2.40, 3.00, 3.60, 4.80 (tax incl.)
EXCLUSIVE ON DECCA RECORDS
PETE KAMERON and HAROLD LEVENTHAL present
America's most popular folk singers
THE WEAVERS
2nd ANNUAL
HOLIDAY
CONCERT
Folk songs around the world
TOWN HALL
TWO PERFORMANCES
Fri. & Sat. Eve., Dec. 21, 22
AT 8:40 P.M.
Tickets: $1.20, $1.80, $2.40, $3.00, $3.60 (Tax incl.)
EXCLUSIVE ON DECCA RECORDS
ONLY NEW YORK APPEARANCE THIS SEASON!
PETE KAMERON & HAROLD LEVENTHAL
Present
America's most popular folk singers
THE WEAVERS
3rd ANNUAL
HOLIDAY
CONCERT
Folk songs around the world
TOWN HALL
TWO PERFORMANCES
Fri. & Sat. Eves. Dec. 26,
AT 8:40 P.M.
Tickets: $1.20, $1.80, $2.40, $3.00, $3.60 (Tax incl.)

The Weavers at Rotary Ann Day, Pasadena, October 15, 1952.

The Weavers' Town Hall Concerts, Christmas 1950–1952.

Hootenanny at Carnegie Hall, sponsored by *Sing Out!* September 16, 1961.

Pete Seeger, "The Midnight Special" concert, Carnegie Hall, February 22, 1958.

"Rally for Trade and Peace with China" ticket, Chicago, April 3, 1954.

THE MUSICAL commies mouth the words, but the Kremlin masterminds call the tune

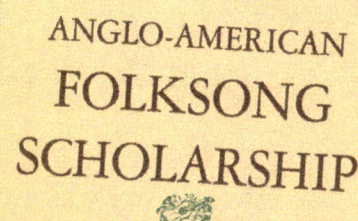

"My Bonnie Lies Over the Ocean" and "On Top of Old Smoky" (Wheaties Red Record, GM 7, ca. 1950).

Red Channels: The Report of Communist Influence in Radio and Television (New York: Counterattack, 1950).

Cartoon from J. B. Matthews, "The Commies Go After the Kids," *American Legion Magazine*, December 1949.

16: Elvis vs. Belafonte, vol. 1, no. 1, July 1957.

D. K. Wilgus, *Anglo-American Folksong Scholarship since 1898* (New Brunswick: Rutgers University Press, 1959).

Teen, vol. 1, no. 2, July 1957.

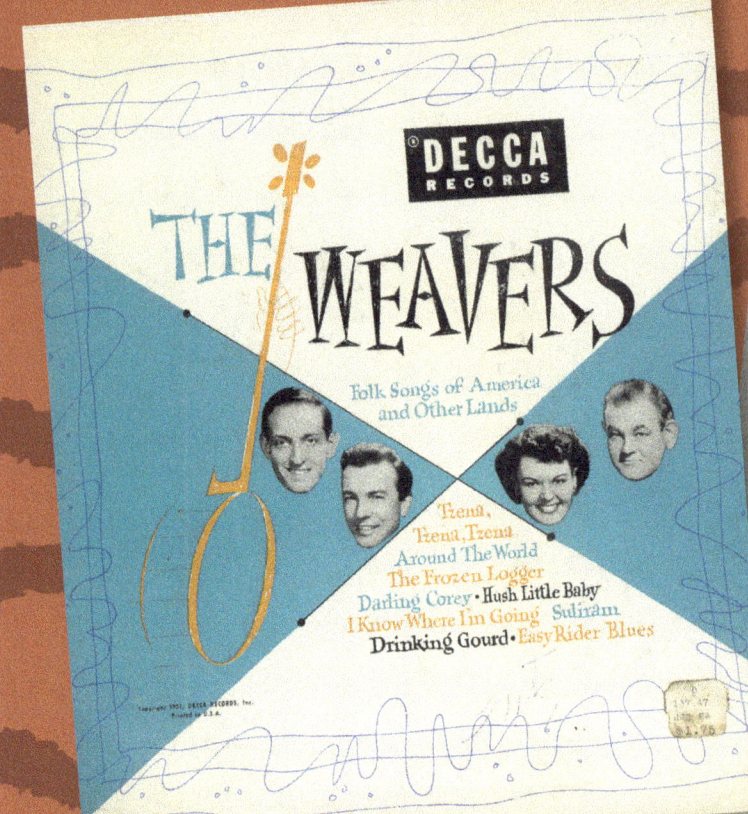

The Weavers, *Folk Songs of America and Other Lands* (Decca Records, DL5285, 1951).

The Weavers, *Sing Folk Songs of America and Other Lands* (New York: Folkways Music Publishers, 1951).

"Hear America Singing with Guy Carawan," flyer, 1956.

"The Songs of Woody Guthrie," flyer, March 17, 1956.

Pete Seeger and Laura Duncan, flyer, March 18, 1955.

"Bob Gibson Sings Offbeat Folksongs," flyer.

Harry Belafonte at the Riviera Hotel, Las Vegas.

Harry Belafonte in the Empire Room, Palmer House, Chicago.

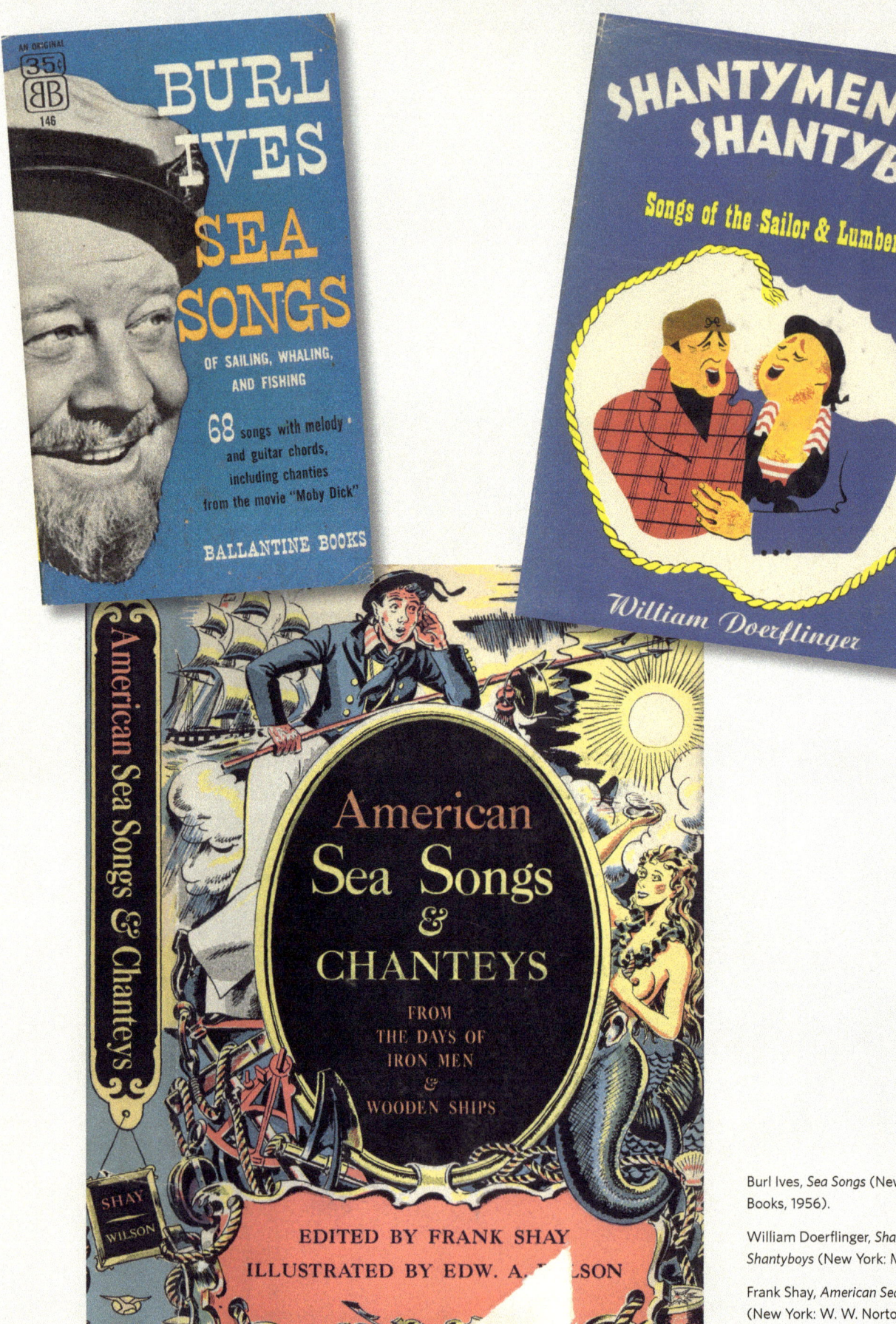

Burl Ives, *Sea Songs* (New York: Ballantine Books, 1956).

William Doerflinger, *Shantymen and Shantyboys* (New York: Macmillan Co., 1951).

Frank Shay, *American Sea Songs & Chanteys* (New York: W. W. Norton & Co., 1948, originally published in 1924 as *Iron Men and Wooden Ships*).

Jean Ritchie, *A Garland of Mountain Song* (New York: Broadcast Music, Inc., 1953).

Carl Sandburg, *New American Songbag* (New York: Broadcast Music, Inc., 1950).

John W. Schaum, *The Folk Song Book* (New York: Belwin, 1955).

Sylvia and John Kolb, *A Treasury of Folk Songs* (New York: Bantam Books, 1954, first published 1948).

Frank Warner Sings American Folk Songs and Ballads (Elektra, ELK 3, 1952).

Malvina Reynolds, *Song in My Pocket* (San Francisco: California Labor School, 1954).

Brownie McGhee Blues (Folkways, FP 30-2, 1955).

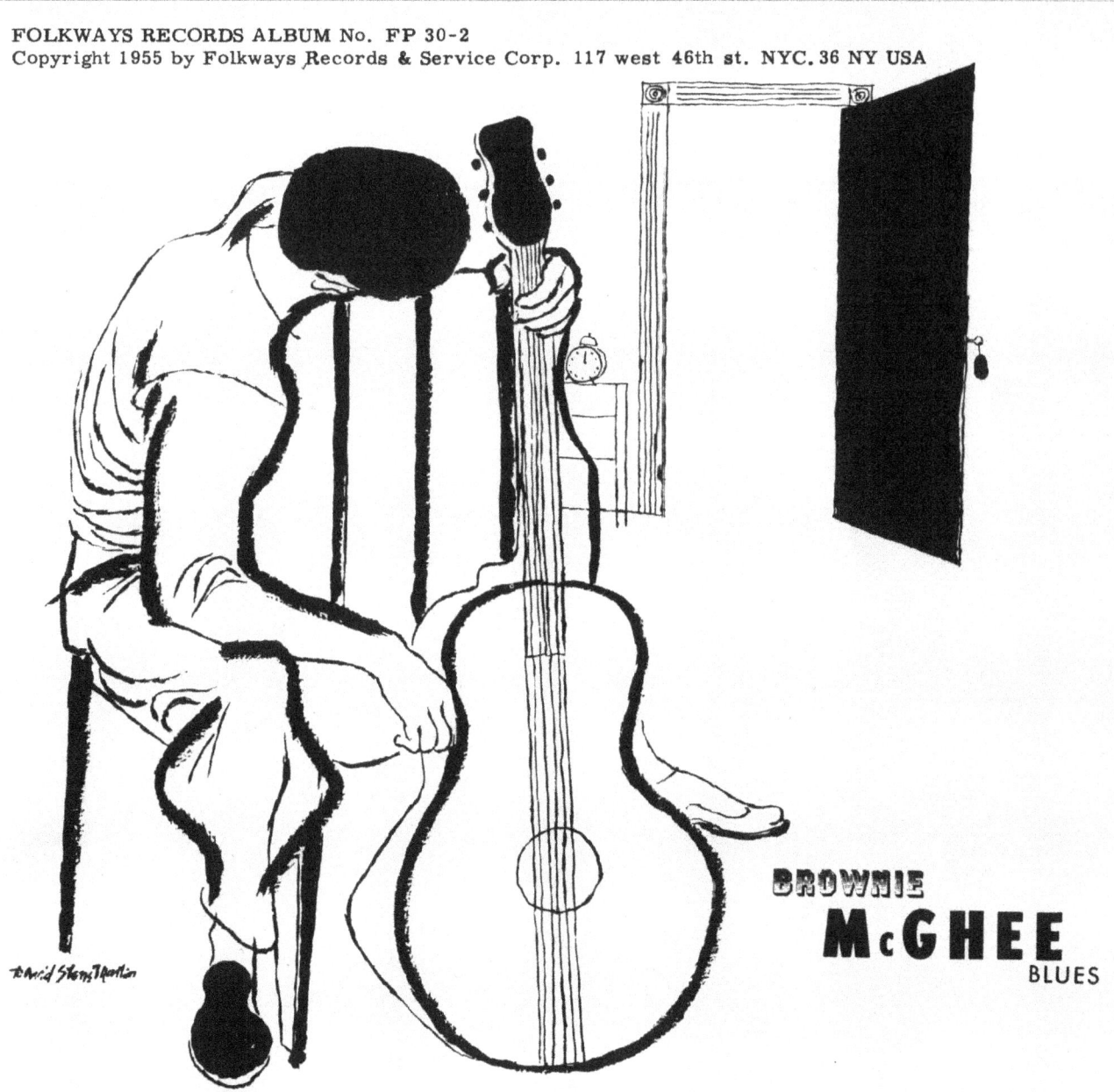

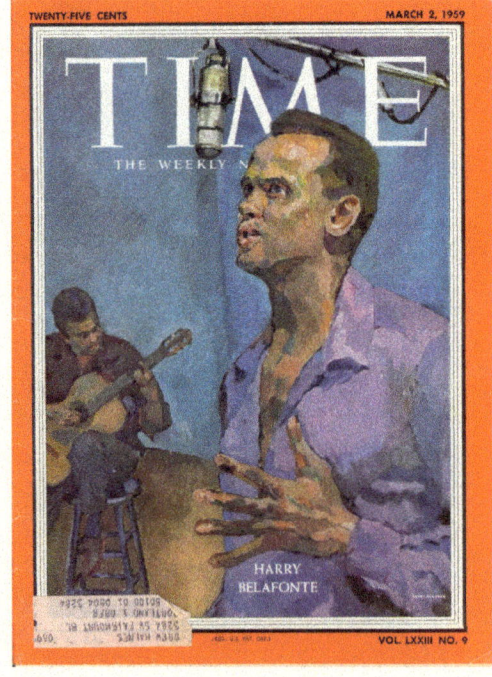

Erik Darling, Bob Carey, and Alan Arkin, "The Banana Boat Song" sheet music, 1956.

Harry Belafonte on cover of *Time*, March 2, 1959.

Lord Burgess, William Attaway, and Harry Belafonte, "Day-O," sheet music, 1955.

Harry Belafonte, *Downbeat*, March 4, 1957.

Harry Belafonte and Lord Burgess, "Island in the Sun," sheet music, 1956.

DAY-O
(BANANA BOAT)
Words and Music by LORD BURGESS, WILLIAM ATTAWAY and HARRY BELAFONTE

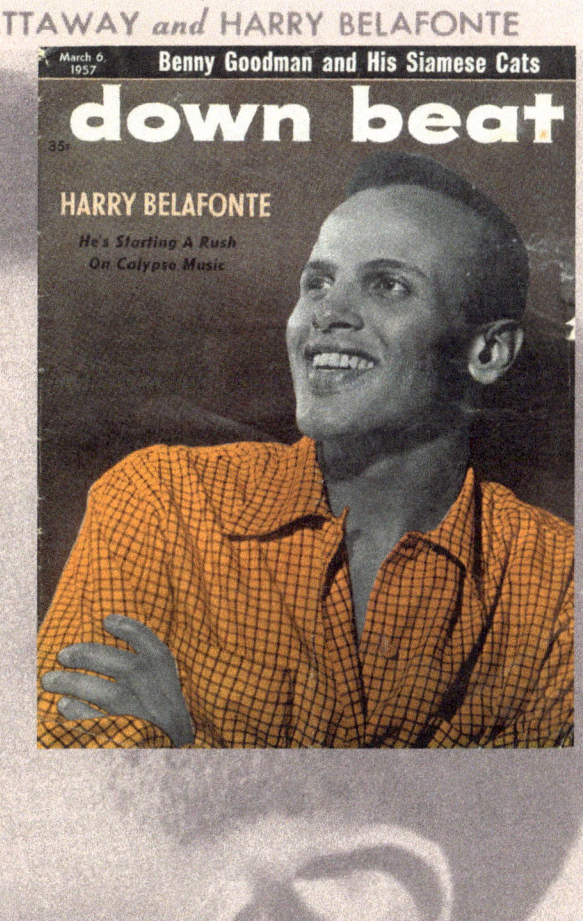

William Attaway, *Calypso Song Book* (New York: McGraw-Hill Co., 1957).

Marianne and Other Calypso Songs You'll Like (Hollywood: Montclare Music Corp., 1957).

Let's All Sing . . . Calypso (New York: Mills Music, Inc., 1957).

Norman Luboff Choir, "Calypso Carnival" label of 16-inch phonograph record transcription (Armed Forces Radio and Television Service, 1950s).

The Tarriers, *Calypso-Land* (New York: Edward B. Marks Music Corp., 1957).

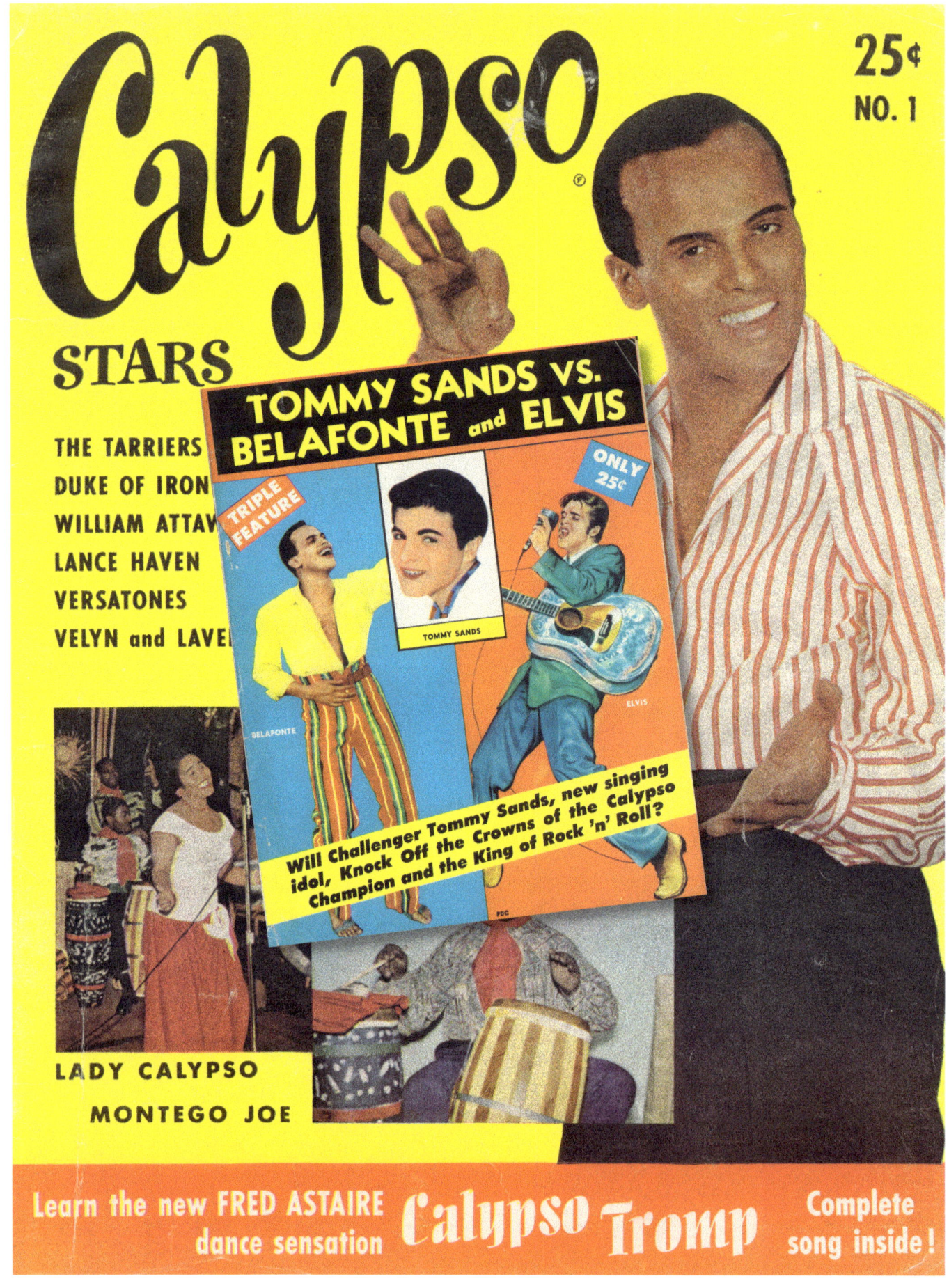

Tommy Sands vs Belafonte and Elvis (New York: The Girl Friend-The Boy Friend Corp., 1957).

Calypso Stars, no. 1, 1957.

Star Calypso Songs, vol. 1, no. 1, 1957.

Calypso Album, 1957.

Harry Belafonte: His Complete Life Story (New York: Hillman Periodicals, 1957).

Calypso, no. 1, 1957.

Calypso Songs, vol. 1, no. 1, July 1957.

Calypso Song Craze, vol. 1, no. 1, May 1957.

Caravan

10¢
APRIL 1958

THE SHANTY BOYS

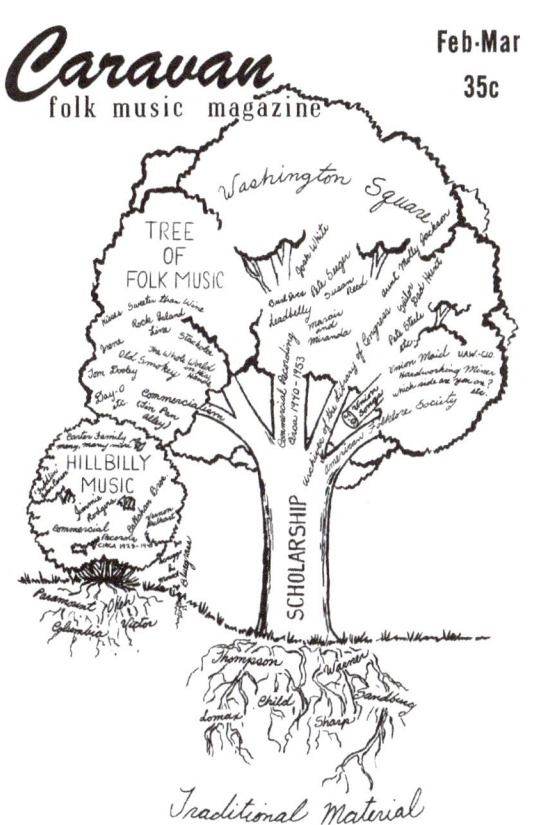

The Shanty Boys on cover of *Caravan*, no. 9, April 1958.

Caravan, no. 15, February–March 1959, with "Tree of Folk Music."

Gardyloo, no. 3, June 1959.

Little Sandy Review, no. 1, March (?) 1960.

Josh White and Ivor Mairants, *The Josh White Guitar Method* (London: Boosey & Hawkes, 1956).

Vega Banjo ad for "Seeger Model," 1960.

Pete Seeger, *How to Play the 5-String Banjo* (Beacon, NY: By the author, 1954).

Alan Lomax and Peggy Seeger, *American Folk Guitar* (New York: Robbins Music Corp., 1957).

Elektra Folk Song Kit (New York: Elektra Corp., 1959).

Folkways Records catalog for Pete Seeger, 1957.

Columbia (Records) Folk Music Catalog, 1952/53.

Israel G. Young, catalog no. 2, 1957.

FOLKWAYS RECORD & SERVICE CORP.
117 West 46th Street, N.Y.C. 36

The World's
LARGEST COLLECTION
of
Authentic Folk Music
on Longplay Records
- Ethnic
- American
- International
- Science
- Literature
- Jazz
- Children

First Annual Newport Folk Festival, program, July 11–12, 1959.

"Four Approaches to Folk Song," program, University of California, Berkeley, September–November 1957.

"American Balladry and Folk Song," program, University of California, Berkeley, 1958.

"A Weekend of Folk Music," program, University of California, Berkeley, June 27–30, 1958.

Cherry Lane Theatre, Swapping Song Fair, flyer, May 12, 1959.

Sing Out! hootenanny program, Carnegie Hall, September 19, 1958.

A Weekend of FOLK MUSIC

on the BERKELEY CAMPUS of the UNIVERSITY OF CALIFORNIA

June 27–30 1958

JOSEF MARAIS AND MIRANDA are famous for their singing of songs of the South African Veld and other lands. They met nearly twenty years ago and have been singing together since. Marais is particularly noted for his translations and adaptations of foreign songs. They are known through their concerts, books, records, and radio and television appearances.

JEAN RITCHIE* comes from a singing Kentucky family, and she sings the songs her family has passed down since before the American Revolution. She accompanies herself on dulcimer and guitar. Her style is simple and unaffected. In addition to concert, radio and television appearances, she is known through her many recordings and her several published song collections.

Both musician and folklorist, SAM HINTON is a popular concert, radio, television, and recording artist. He teaches folk music courses for both the University of California Extension and the Idyllwild School of Music and Arts. He has recorded a number of songs for the Archives of Folk Song at the Library of Congress. His specialty is American and Irish folk songs, his style simple and straightforward.

FRANK WARNER* is a leading folk singer and collector of American folk music. He has collected throughout North Carolina, New York, New Hampshire, Massachusetts, and other Eastern areas. He sings his songs as he learned them, in a rough, unchanged style, accompanying himself on banjo and guitar. His work on records and in concerts is widely known, particularly in the East.

Spanish, Mexican, and Gypsy songs and dances are the specialty of MARGARITA and CLARK ALLEN. While Margarita performs authentic dances learned in the areas of their origin, Clark accompanies her on the guitar. Folk songs and flamenco singing are offered by Clark as he accompanies himself and Margarita on the *gaita*, a Spanish bagpipe; *tambori*, a drum; *txistu*, a shrill three-hole flute; *bandurria*, a twelve-string instrument; and lute.

ANDREW ROWAN SUMMERS* grew up in the highlands of Virginia, an area rich in folklore. He has been singing and collecting ballads and folk songs in the East for many years and is now a leading ballad singer and accomplished dulcimer player. He is prominent in the East through his concerts and records.

BILLY FAIER has traveled across America "with his banjo on his knee." His forte is the five string banjo. He has collected hundreds of songs which he sings to the banjo accompaniment or plays on banjo alone. He is regularly heard in the Bay Area over KPFA-FM and in addition is a concert, television, and recording artist.

*First Bay Area appearance.

BARRY OLIVIER *is adviser to the Committee on Drama, Lectures* ...

SPECIAL SOUVENIR SUPPLEMENT

hootenanny

A SING OUT PRODUCTION

PETE SEEGER

WILL GEER

HALLY WOOD

BOB CAREY

JERRY SILVERMAN

friday sept. 19 1958

CARNEGIE HALL

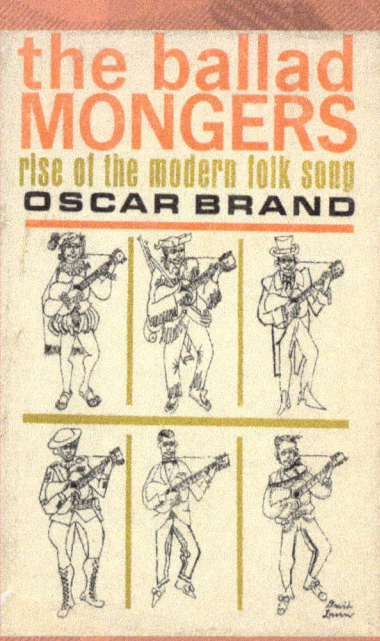

Highwaymen, *Folk Song Album* (Miami Beach, FL: Hansen Publications, 1962).

Harold Courlander, *Negro Folk Music U.S.A.* (New York: Columbia University Press, 1963).

The Journeymen songbook (New York: Hansen Publishing, 1965).

Oscar Brand, *The Ballad Mongers* (New York: Funk and Wagnalls, 1962).

Kingston Trio on cover of *Life*, August 3, 1959.

Kingston Trio on cover of *Rogue* magazine, October 1960.

Howard Grafman and B. T. Manning, *Folk Music USA* (New York: Citadel Press, 1962).

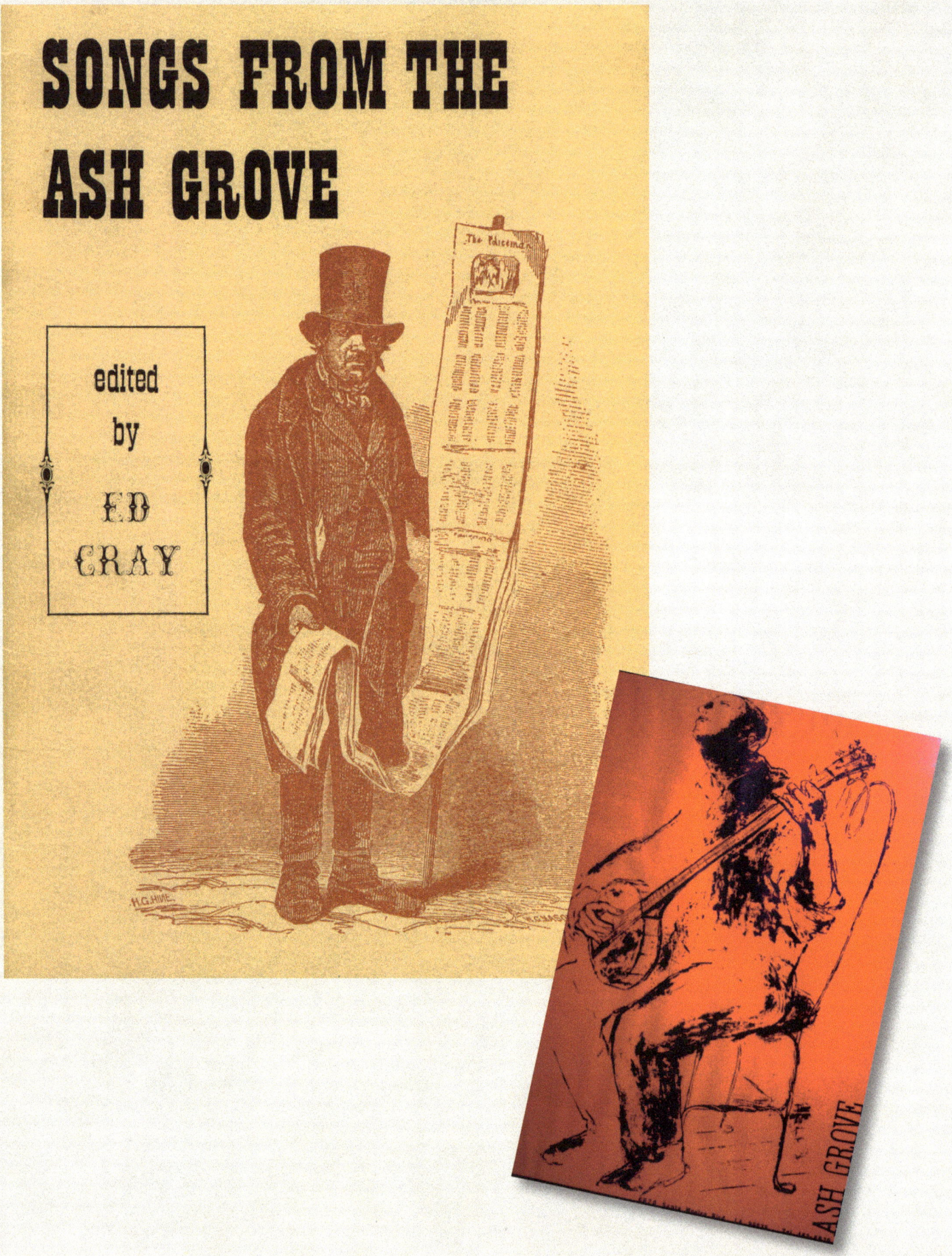

Ed Cray, ed., *Songs from the Ash Grove* (Los Angeles: Ash Grove, 1959).

Ash Grove (Los Angeles) poster, 1965.

Brian Bird, *Skiffle: The Story of Folk Song with a Jazz Beat* (London: Robert Hale Ltd., 1958).

John A. Lomax and Alan Lomax, *The Leadbelly Legend* (New York: Folkways Music Publishers, 1959; revised edition, 1965).

Folk Songs at Columbia University with Tom Glazer et al., concert flyer, March 18, 1960.

Folk Music Guide USA, Izzy Young's Folklore Center, New York, October 14, 1959.

Folksingers Guild Presents Folkmusic at Midnight, concert flyer, April 25, 1958.

Gerdes Folk City, New York, concert schedule.

"All for Pete!" concert flyer, San Francisco, May 12, 1961.

"All Over This Land," concert flyer, Los Angeles.

Folkway Concert Series, flyer, New York.

Folklore Center, concert flyer, March 7, 1957.

Calypso Steel Band Clash, concert flyer, New York, September 29, 1956.

Greenwich Village Story, lobby card (Lion International, 1963).

The Young Swingers, movie poster (Associated Producers, 1963).

The Legend of Tom Dooley, lobby card (Columbia Pictures, 1959).

Al Compas del Calypso, lobby card, 1957 (Mexican release of *Calypso Heat Wave* [Clover Productions, 1957]).

Greenwich Village Story, movie poster, 1963.

Calypso Joe, lobby card (Allied Artists, 1957).

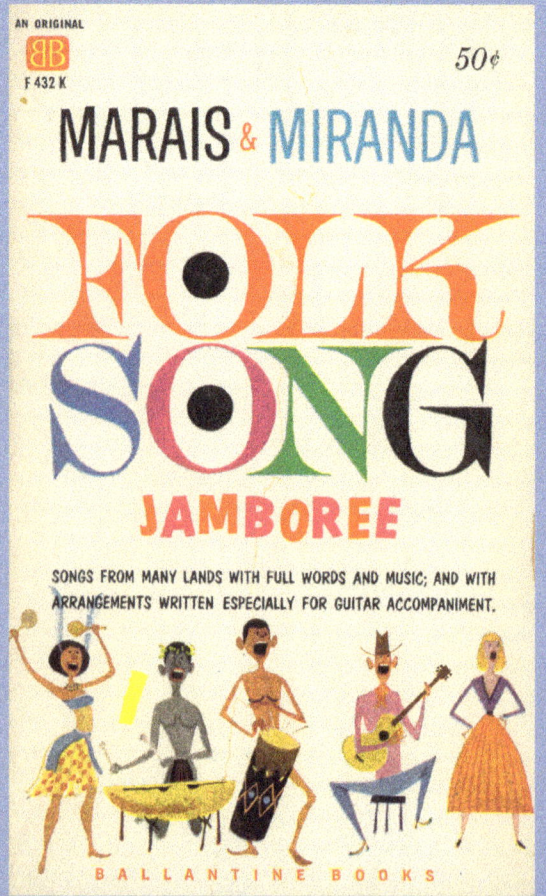

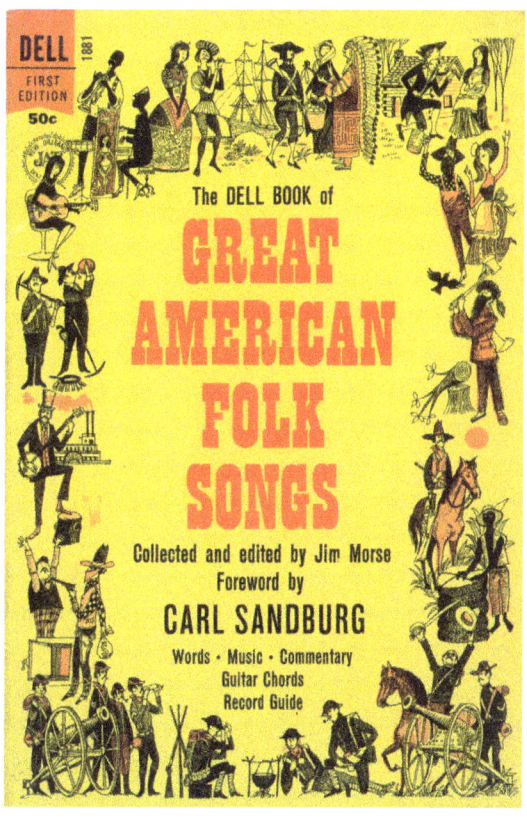

Tom Glazer, *A New Treasury of Folk Songs* (New York: Bantam Books, 1961).

Herbert Haufrecht, *Folksing* (New York: Berkley Publishing Co., 1960).

Oscar Brand, *Bawdy Songs and Backroom Ballads* (New York: Caravelle Books, 1960).

Marais & Miranda, *Folk Song Jamboree* (New York: Ballantine Books, 1960).

Oscar Brand, *Folk Songs for Fun* (New York: Berkley Pub. Co., 1961).

Jim Morse, *The Dell Book of Great American Folk Songs* (New York: Dell Pub., Co., 1963).

Marais & Miranda, *World Folk Songs* (New York: Ballantine Books, 1964).

ASUC Program

SAM HINTON
FOLK SONG CONCERT
SATURDAY, OCTOBER 13 * 8:30 P.M. * PAULEY BALLROOM

MARC ET ANDRE
TUESDAY, OCTOBER 16 * 8:30 P.M. * PAULEY BALLROOM

BARBARA DANE
SATURDAY, OCTOBER 20 • 8:30 P.M. • PAULEY BALLROOM

KARL WOLFRAM GERMAN LUTENIST SINGER
TUESDAY, OCTOBER 23 * 8:30 P.M. * PAULEY BALLROOM

RAMBLIN' JACK ELLIOTT
FOLK SONG CONCERT
SATURDAY, OCTOBER 27 * 8:30 P.M. * PAULEY BALLROOM

DUKE ELLINGTON AND HIS BAND
MONDAY, NOVEMBER 12 • 8:30 P.M. • HARMON GYM

THE KINGSTON TRIO
BIG GAME CONCERT
TUESDAY, NOVEMBER 20 ★ 8:30 P.M. ★ HARMON GYM

WINTER FOLK MUSIC FESTIVAL
SAM HINTON ★ JEAN RITCHIE
The Greenbriar Boys and a Staff of Ten Folk Song Artists!
NOVEMBER 25 TO DECEMBER 2
CONCERTS WORKSHOPS INFORMAL EVENTS

SPECIAL CHILDREN'S CHRISTMAS CONCERT OF FOLK SONG SAM HINTON
SATURDAY, DECEMBER 22 * 10:30 A.M. * PAULEY BALLROOM

FOLK SONG JAM SESSION
Every Saturday Night, 9 p.m. - 1 a.m. BEAR'S LAIR, STUDENT CENTER
Bill Petrocelli in charge Sponsored by the ASUC Union Program Board

SUNDAY NIGHT FILMS
7:30 p.m. Sunday Evenings in the PAULEY BALLROOM
Sponsored by the ASUC Union Program Board

FRIDAY NIGHT CABARETS
Every Friday Night, 9 p.m. - 1 a.m. BEAR'S LAIR, STUDENT CENTER
Sponsored by the ASUC Union Program Board

For kind assistance in announcing the appearance of
The Royal Scots Greys & Argylls
we are indebted to
Scottish Imports, Ltd., 374 Geary St., San Francisco
and the CALEDONIAN CLUB of San Francisco

A.S.U.C. MAILING LIST CARD

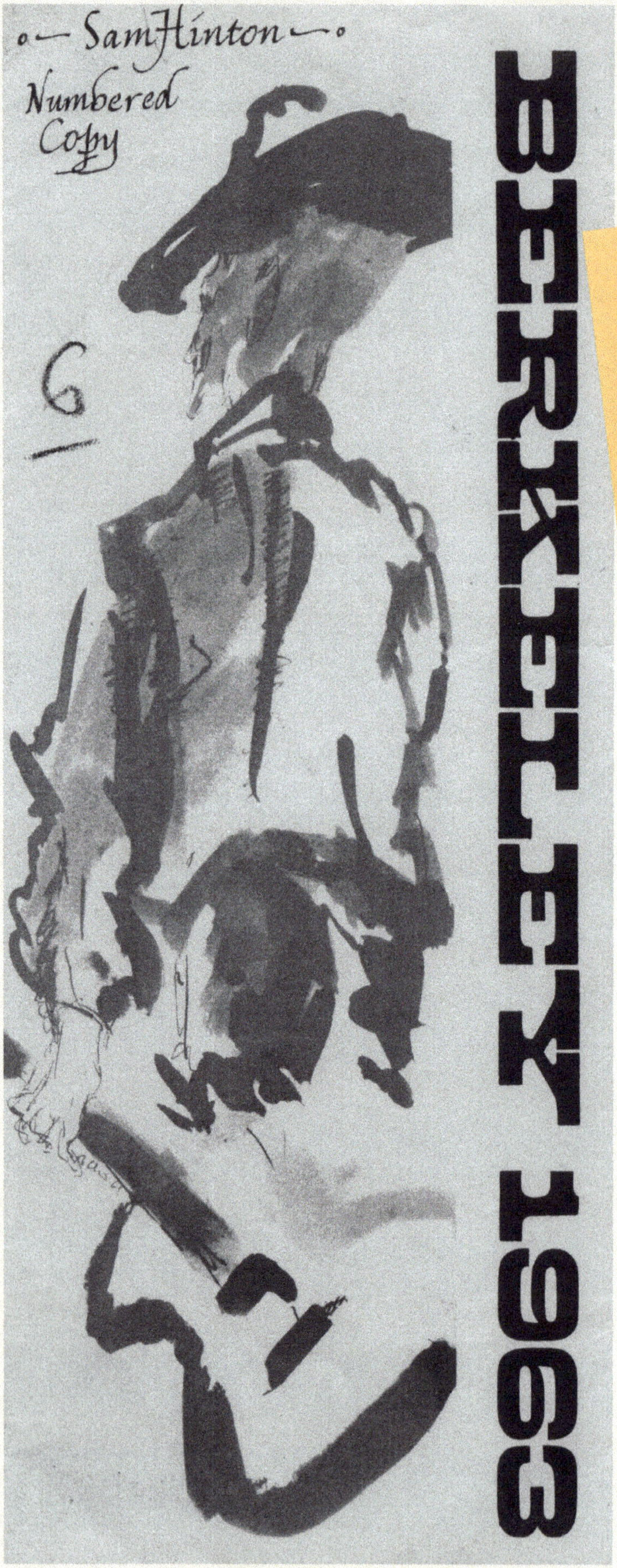

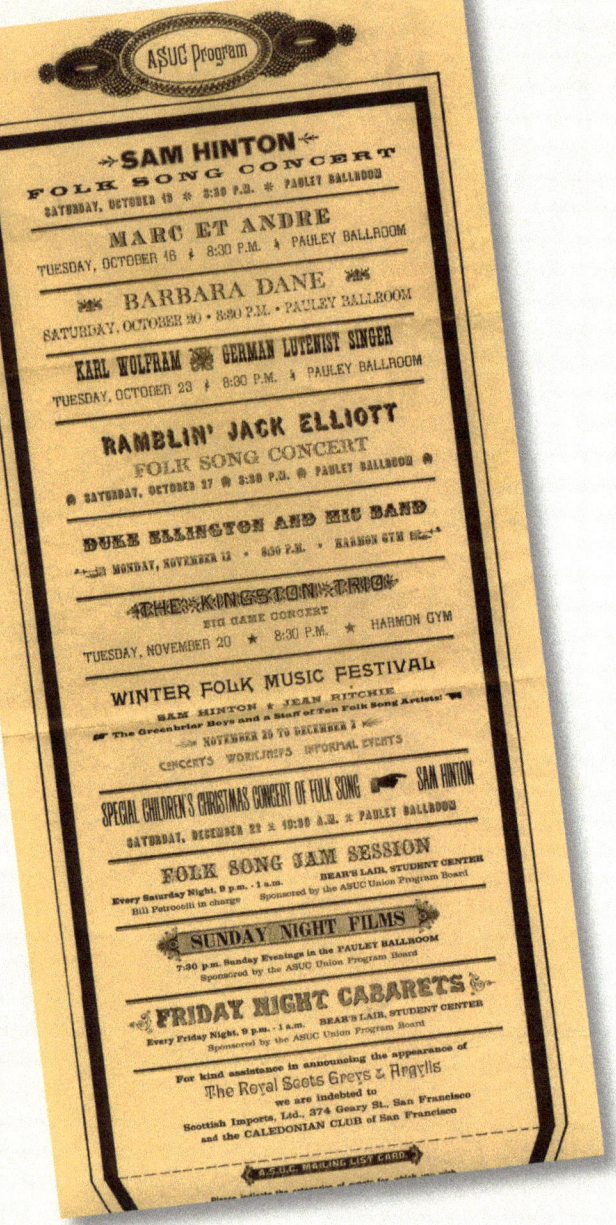

Sixth Annual Berkeley Folk Music Festival, program, June 26–30, 1963.

Notice of concerts, University of California, Berkeley, Fall 1962.

The Friends of Old Time Music, concert flyer, February 11, 1961.

Colorado Folk Festival, program, Denver, October–November 1960.

New Lost City Ramblers/Elizabeth Cotten, concert flyer, December 23, 1960.

Bob Dylan on cover of *Sing Out!* vol. 12, no. 4, October–November 1962.

Peter, Paul and Mary on Tour (New York: Pepamar Music Corp., 1964).

The Kingston Trio (New York: Random House, 1960).

Gordo comic strip, 1962 (Fall River Music, Inc.).

Folk singers wear Wranglers

A pair of jeans, smoked glasses and a guitar. They're as much a part of his repertoire as "Down in the Valley." Take one of them away and you take away his character. Jeans are standard equipment with a lot of unusual people. And Wranglers are the jeans they choose. We can't guarantee you a split week at Nashville, Tennessee; but you can have the same lean, slim fit, the same sure-sizing that any folk singer wants. Pre-shrunk to the right size before they're even sewn together. In sizes for all the folk singers in your family. From **$2.49 to $4.29**.

WRANGLERS
A DIVISION OF BLUE BELL INC.
In Canada W. F. Howick Mfgr. Co., Ltd., Montreal

I.U. FOLKSONG CLUB presents
DOC WATSON
Outstanding Traditional Guitarist and Folk Music Performer
Recorded on Folkways and Vanguard Records
SATURDAY, MARCH 20, 1965
8:00 P.M.
Admission: Members $1.25 / Non-Members $1.50
WHITTENBERGER AUDITORIUM

I.U. FOLKSONG CLUB Presents
DAVE VAN RONK
Singing
Blues and Ballads
Whittenberger Auditorium
Friday, November 20, 8:00 P.M.

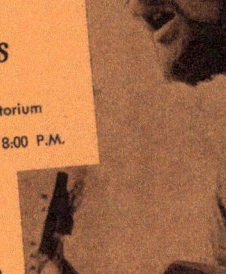

$1.50

SATURDAY NOVEMBER 23 AT 8:00 PM
Lincoln Hall Theater
THE CAMPUS FOLKSONG CLUB
HEDY WEST
MOUNTAIN SONGS & BALLADS
$1.50 ILLINI UNION BOX OFFICE

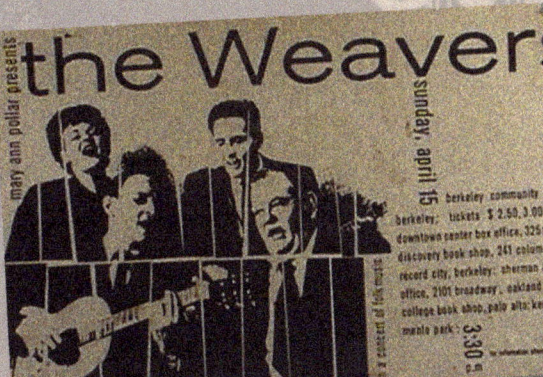

Doc Watson, concert flyer, Indiana University Folksong Club, March 20, 1965.

Dave Van Ronk, concert flyer, Indiana University Folksong Club, November 20, 1964.

"Folk Singers Wear Wranglers," advertisement for Wrangler jeans, *Life*, October 19, 1962.

Hedy West, concert flyer, University of Illinois Campus Folksong Club, November 23, 1963.

The Weavers, concert flyer, Berkeley, April 15, 1962.

Stoneman Family, concert flyer, University of Illinois Campus Folksong Club, May 18, 1963.

Barbara Dane, concert flyer, University of California, Berkeley, March 15, 1963.

The Weavers, concert flyer, Berkeley, November 1, 1963.

Woody Guthrie, *Ballads of Sacco & Vanzetti*, eds. Moses Asch and Irwin Silber (New York: Oak Publications, 1960).

Lee Hays and Pete Seeger, "If I Had a Hammer" sheet music, 1963, printed in Great Britain.

Sing Out! vol. 1, no. 1, May 1950.

How many ears must one man have
Before he can hear people cry?
How many deaths will it take 'til he knows
That too many people have died?
The answer, my friend, is blowin' in the wind,
The answer is blowin' in the wind.'

*© M. Witmark and Sons

Peter, Paul and Mary
SING
"Blowin' in the Wind"

 WARNER BROS. RECORDS
SINGLE NUMBER 5368

Introducing...
BROADSIDE #1 Feb., 1962
Box 193 Cathedral Sta. NYC 25
Price . . . . . . 35¢

BROADSIDE
a handful of songs about our times

Topical songs have been an important part of America's music since early Colonial days. Many people throughout the country today are writing topical songs, and the only way to find out if a song is good is to give it wide circulation and let the singers and listeners decide for themselves. BROADSIDE'S aim is not so much to select and decide as to circulate as many songs as possible and get them out as quickly as possible. Our schedule calls for twice-a-month publication -- this will depend mainly on the contributing songwriters. BROADSIDE may never publish a song that could be called a "folk song." But let us remember that many of our best folk songs were topical songs at their inception. Few would deny the beauty and lasting value of some of Woody Guthrie's songs. Old or new, "a good song can only do good."

HAROLD LEVENTHAL MANAGEMENT, INC.
200 WEST 57TH STREET, NEW YORK 19, N.Y. · JUDSON 6-6553
HAROLD LEVENTHAL
ARLINE CUNNINGHAM · CHARLES CLOSE

NEWS

FOR RELEASE FRIDAY, SEPTEMBER 6, 1963

PETE SEEGER REFUSES TO SIGN "LOYALTY OATH"
FOR THE AMERICAN BROADCASTING COMPANY
TO APPEAR ON HOOTENANNY TV SHOW

Several weeks ago, just as Pete Seeger was leaving for the west coast to begin his world wide concert tour, I was advised that the American Broadcasting Company would "consider Pete Seeger for the ABC Hootenanny Show if he would sign a "loyalty oath affidavit." Because of his tremendously busy schedule and the pressure in leaving for the world tour, Pete Seeger asked me upon my return to New York from the west coast, to advise the ABC network of his reply. Pete Seeger has issued the following statement-

"I have just finished fighting a seven year court battle to prove the principle that such oaths are unconstitutional and I was acquitted and vindicated."

Pete Seeger

It is apparent that the ABC TV network is continuing a blacklisting policy against the appearance of Pete Seeger and the Weavers on the Hootenanny TV show.

HAROLD LEVENTHAL
Representative for
Pete Seeger and The Weavers

# # # # #

Calendar for the Cabale Coffee House, Berkeley, California, June 1964.

Billboard ad for Peter, Paul and Mary, "Blowin' in the Wind," 1963.

Broadside, no. 1, February 1962.

Harold Leventhal, press release, September 6, 1963.

2nd Annual Newport Folk Festival, program, June 24–26, 1960.

Notice of Bob Dylan concert at Carnegie Chapter Hall, New York, presented by the Folklore Center, November 4, 1961.

"For the Love of Pete and Freedom," flyer, Los Angeles, October 6, 1961.

Harry Belafonte with Miriam Makeba, program, Carter Baron Amphitheater, Washington, DC, ca. 1960.

M. A. GREENHILL presents
in the Folklore Concert Series

BROWNIE McGHEE & SONNY TERRY
REV. GARY DAVIS,
BARBARA DANE,
JOHNNY HAMMOND,
ERIC VON SCHMIDT

REALLY SING THE BLUES

JOHN HANCOCK HALL

FRIDAY, JAN. 8 — 8:30 P.M.

Send mail orders with stamped self-addressed envelope to:
Folklore productions, P.O. Box 227, Boston 1.

BRANDEIS UNIVERSITY
2ND ANNUAL FOLK FESTIVAL
SATURDAY, APRIL 25, 1964 at BRANDEIS UNIV., WALTHAM

EVENING CONCERT • 8 P.M. TICKETS: $2.25

- REV. GARY DAVIS
- GEORGIA SEA ISLAND SINGERS & DANCERS with BESSIE JONES
- ROSCOE HOLCOMB
- JIM KWESKIN & THE JUG BAND
- NEW LOST CITY RAMBLERS

AFTERNOON EVENTS

CHILDREN'S CONCERT 1 PM • $1.00
REV. GARY DAVIS
IRENE KOSSOY
TONY SALETAN

FILMS 1 PM • 50¢
HAZARD, KENTUCKY COAL MINERS
and
"TO HEAR MY BANJO PLAY" with PETE SEEGER

GUITAR WORKSHOP 3 PM • 50¢

ALL KINDS-A BLUEGRASS 3 PM • $1.00
CHARLES RIVER VALLEY BOYS
LILLY BROS. & DON STOVER
NEW LOST CITY RAMBLERS

ORDER COUPON
☐ $2.25 ☐ $1.00
ENCLOSED, FIND CHECK MONEY ORDER FOR $___
(I AM ENCLOSING A SELF-ADDRESSED STAMPED ENVELOPE.)
NAME _____
ADDRESS _____
CITY _____ ZONE ___ STATE ___

MAIL ORDERS FROM:
BRANDEIS FOLK FESTIVAL
BRANDEIS UNIVERSITY
WALTHAM, MASS.
OR
FOLKLORE PRODUCTIONS
P.O. BOX 227
BOSTON, MASS. • KU 2-1827

COMMITTEE for MINERS

presents

FOLK MUSIC for HAZARD

Benefit for Unemployed Hazard, Kentucky Coal Miners

Polytechnic Auditorium
Baltimore, Maryland

February 28, 1965

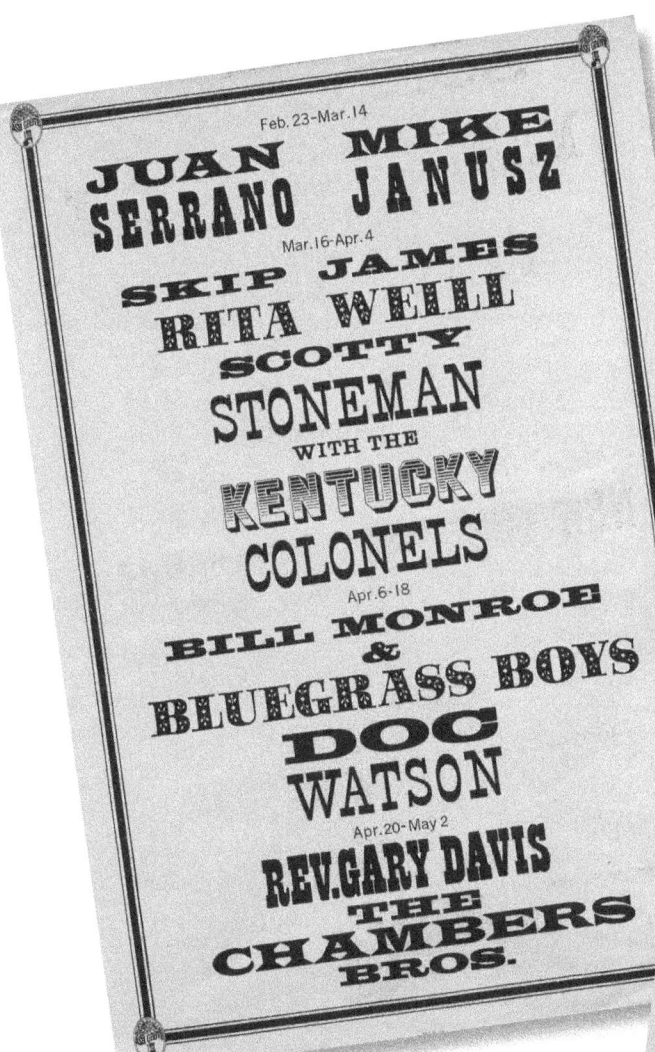

Concert at John Hancock Hall, flyer, Boston, January 8, 1965.

Brandeis University 2nd Annual Folk Festival, flyer, April 25, 1964.

Program for Folk Music for Hazard, Kentucky, coal miners, Baltimore, Maryland, February 28, 1965, with Phil Ochs, Tom Paxton, Buffy Sainte-Marie, Patrick Sky, Jim & Jean, Alix Dobkin, and the Greenbriar Boys.

"Hoot!" Ash Grove, Los Angeles, flyer, July 30–August 18, 1963.

Ash Grove, Los Angeles, flyers for coming concerts, 1963 (?).

Hootenanny ABC-TV, paper dolls, 1964 (front and back of package).

Hootenanny bath powder mitt, Fuller Brush Company, 1964.

Bally Hootenanny pinball machine, flyer, 1964.

Oscar Brand's Authentic Hootenanny Song Book (New York: Alfred Music Co., 1963).

Hootenanny candy bar wrapper, "An Old Time Favorite," 1964.

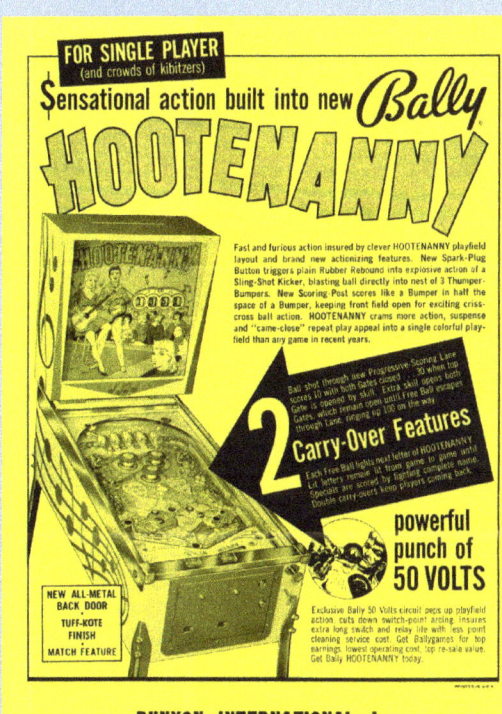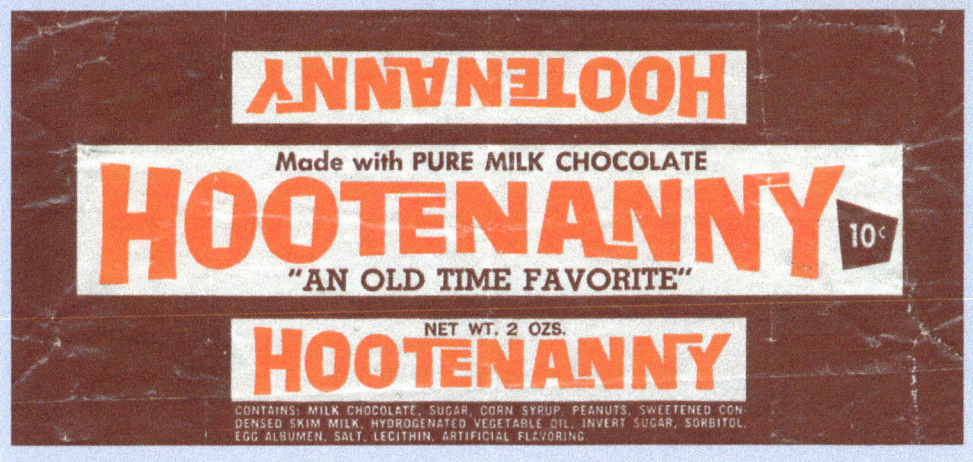

Batman comic guest-starring the Hootenanny Hotshots, no. 164 (National Periodical Publications, Inc., June 1964), cover and inside page.

William Steuart McBirnie, *Songs of Subversion* (Glendale, CA: A Voice of American Publication, 1965).

David A. Noebel, *Rhythm, Riots and Revolution* (Tulsa, OK: Christian Crusade Publications, 1966).

Love Diary (Charlton Comics Group, September 1966), cover and inside page.

George Goehring, Eddie V. Deane, and Peg Horther, "Hootenanny," sheet music, 1963.

Mort Gerberg cartoons, *Hootenanny*, vol. 1, no. 2, March 1964.

Hootenanny, vol. 1, no. 2, March 1964.

Hootenanny Hoot, movie poster (Four-Leaf Productions, 1963).

Alfred Uhry and Richard Lewine, "Hootenanny Saturday Night," sheet music, 1963.

Hootenanny Hoot, movie lobby card, 1963.

"Hoot" Kit! Song Book (Los Angeles: Cal Music Press, 1963).

Hootenanny, vol. 1, no. 3, May 1964.

Peter, Paul and Mary on cover of *Hootenanny*, vol. 1, no. 1, December 1963.

113

Orange Crush Hootenanny Party Kit, 1964, two items.

Orange Crush Hootenanny Party Kit, poster, 1964.

Hootenanny Sing! (New York: Hollis Music, Inc., ca. 1963).

American Hootenanny: Reprints from Sing Out! The Folk Song Magazine (New York: Consolidated Music Pub., 1964).

James F. Leisy, *Hootenanny Tonight!* (Greenwich, CT: Gold Medal Books, 1964).

Hootenanny Song Book: Reprints from Sing Out! The Folk Song Magazine (New York: Consolidated Music Pub., 1963).

Palmer-Hughes *Hootenanny* accordion instruction book (New York: Alfred Music, 1964).

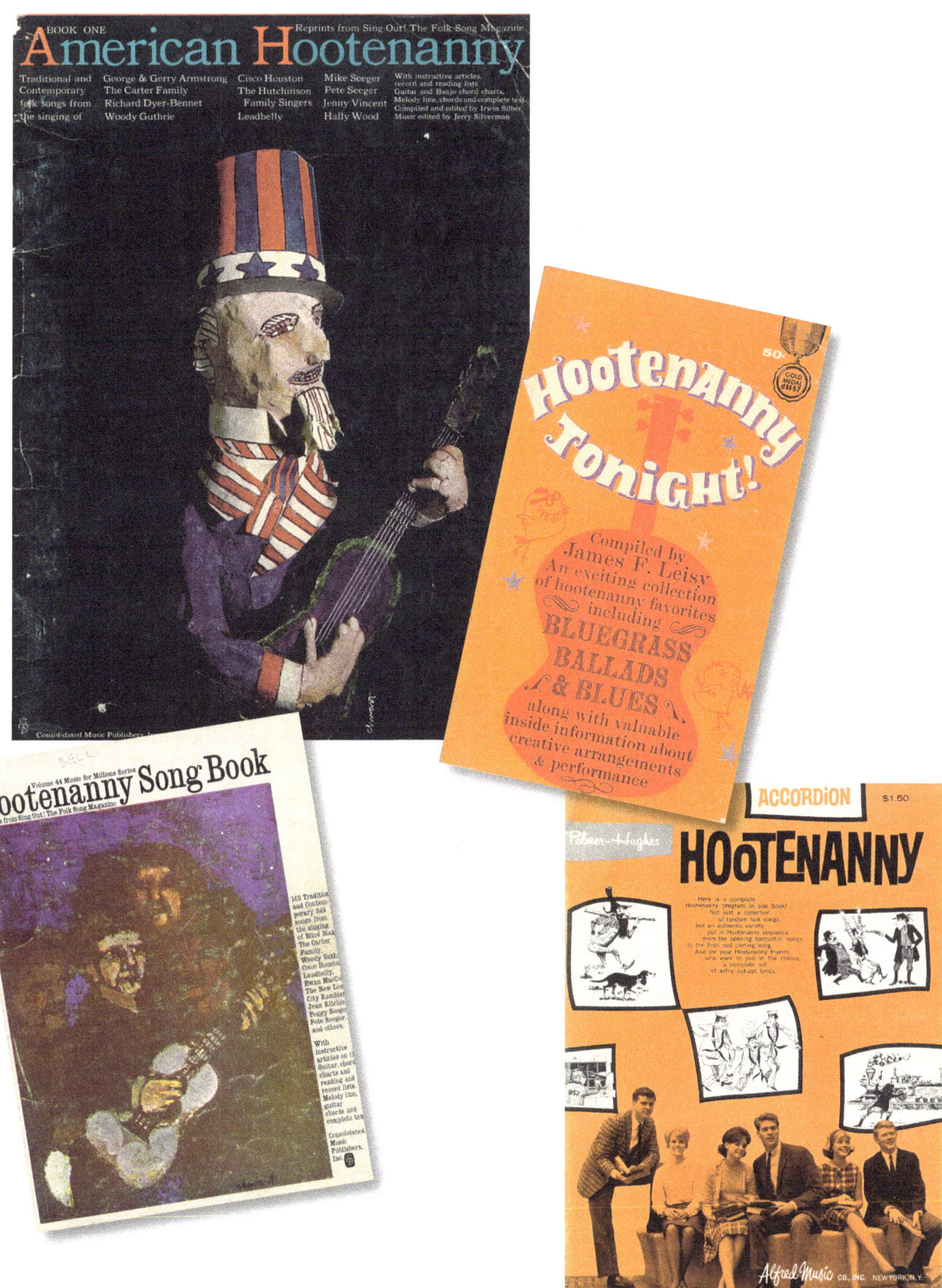

ABC-TV Hootenanny Show, vol. 1, no. 1, January 1964.

ABC-TV Hootenanny Show, vol. 1, no. 3, July 1964.

ABC-TV Hootenanny Folk Songs, vol. 1, no. 1, 1964.

Hootenanny Hoot, advertisement, 1963.

Hootenanny Songs and Stars, vol. 1, no. 1, Winter 1964.

Hootenanny Hoot, movie poster (Metro-Goldwyn-Mayer, 1963).

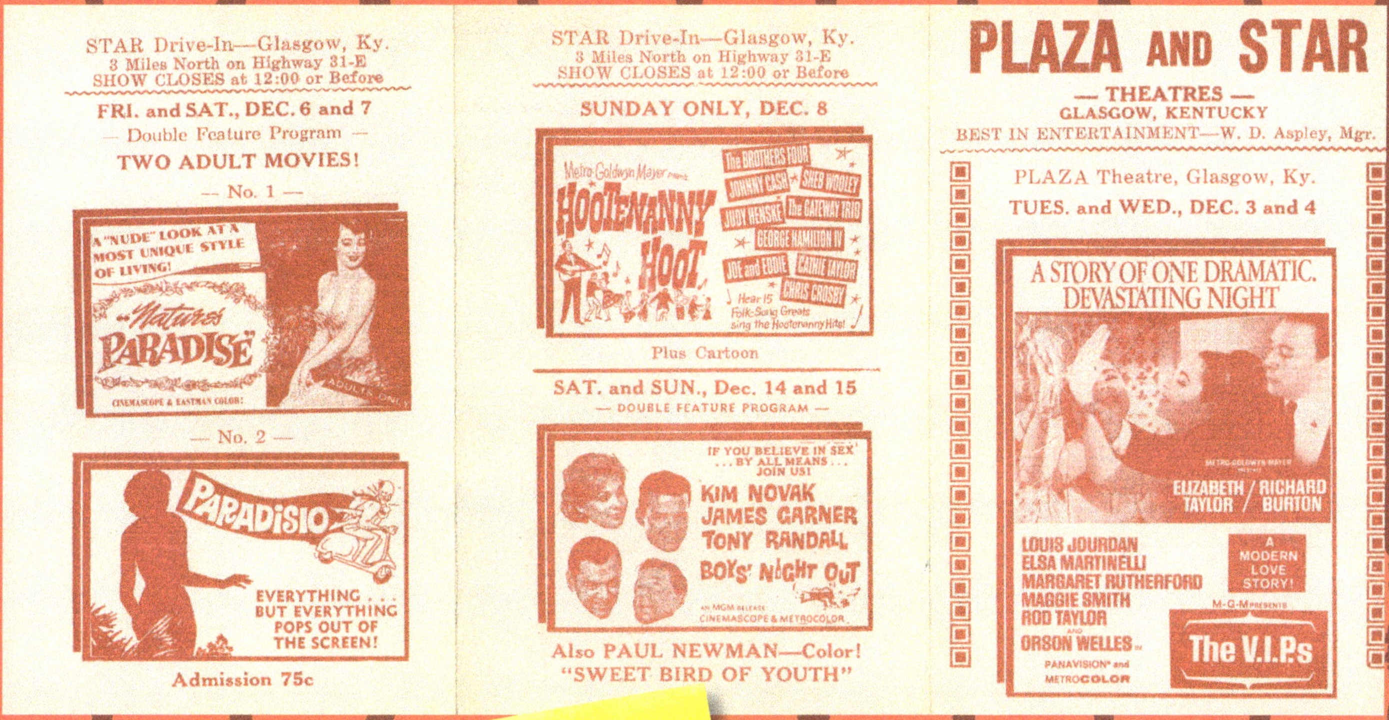
STAR Drive-In—Glasgow, Ky.
3 Miles North on Highway 31-E
SHOW CLOSES at 12:00 or Before
FRI. and SAT., DEC. 6 and 7
— Double Feature Program —
TWO ADULT MOVIES!
— No. 1 —
A "NUDE" LOOK AT A MOST UNIQUE STYLE OF LIVING!
Nature's PARADISE
— No. 2 —
PARADISIO
EVERYTHING... BUT EVERYTHING POPS OUT OF THE SCREEN!
Admission 75c
STAR Drive-In—Glasgow, Ky.
3 Miles North on Highway 31-E
SHOW CLOSES at 12:00 or Before
SUNDAY ONLY, DEC. 8
Metro-Goldwyn-Mayer presents
HOOTENANNY HOOT
The BROTHERS FOUR
JOHNNY CASH
SHEB WOOLEY
JUDY HENSKE
The GATEWAY TRIO
GEORGE HAMILTON IV
JOE and EDDIE
CATHIE TAYLOR
CHRIS CROSBY
Hear 15 Folk-Song Greats sing the Hootenanny Hits!
Plus Cartoon
SAT. and SUN., Dec. 14 and 15
— DOUBLE FEATURE PROGRAM —
IF YOU BELIEVE IN SEX ... BY ALL MEANS ... JOIN US!
KIM NOVAK
JAMES GARNER
TONY RANDALL
BOYS' NIGHT OUT
CINEMASCOPE & METROCOLOR
Also PAUL NEWMAN—Color!
"SWEET BIRD OF YOUTH"
PLAZA AND STAR
— THEATRES —
GLASGOW, KENTUCKY
BEST IN ENTERTAINMENT—W. D. Aspley, Mgr.
PLAZA Theatre, Glasgow, Ky.
TUES. and WED., DEC. 3 and 4
A STORY OF ONE DRAMATIC, DEVASTATING NIGHT
ELIZABETH TAYLOR / RICHARD BURTON
LOUIS JOURDAN
ELSA MARTINELLI
MARGARET RUTHERFORD
MAGGIE SMITH
ROD TAYLOR
ORSON WELLES
A MODERN LOVE STORY!
M-G-M PRESENTS
The V.I.Ps
PANAVISION and METROCOLOR

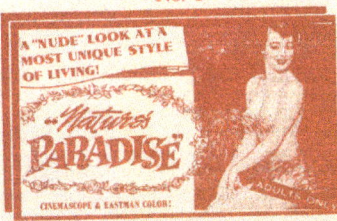

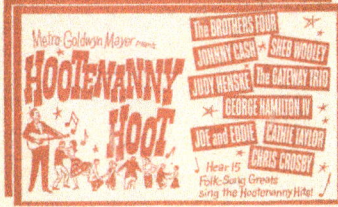

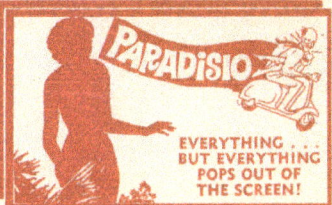

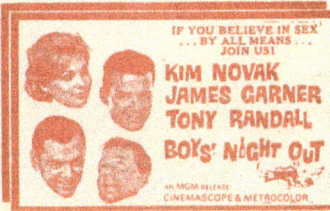

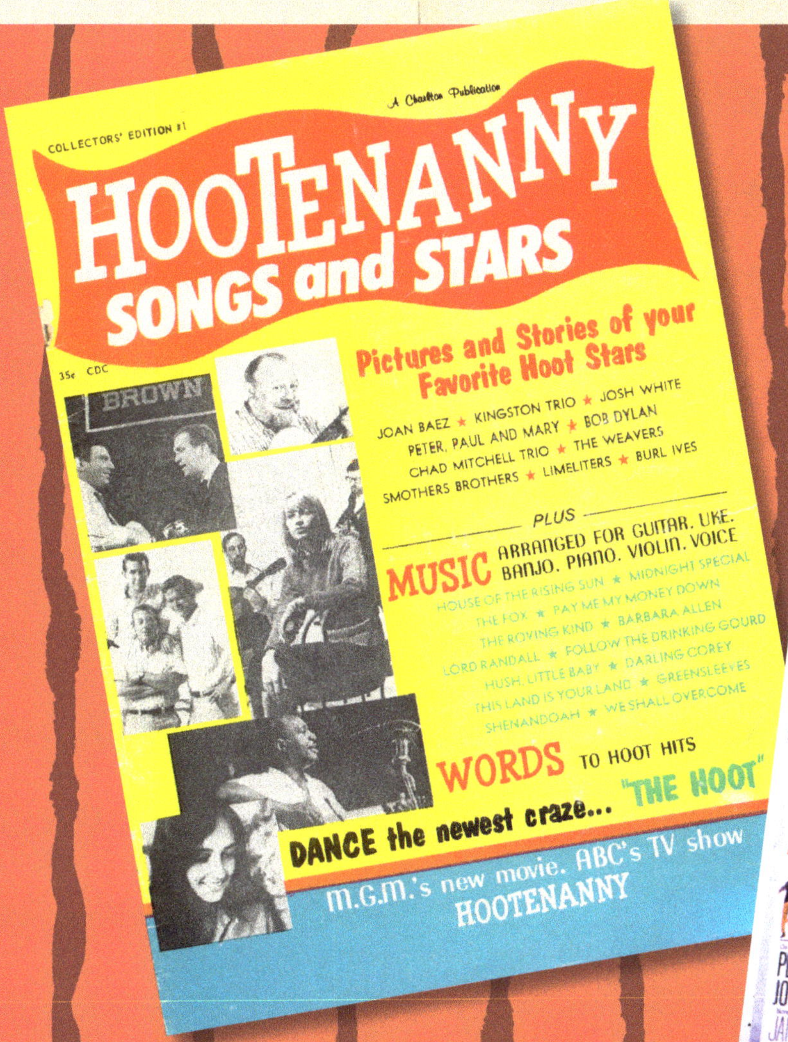
COLLECTORS' EDITION #1
A Charlton Publication
HOOTENANNY SONGS and STARS
35¢ CDC
Pictures and Stories of your Favorite Hoot Stars
JOAN BAEZ ★ KINGSTON TRIO ★ JOSH WHITE
PETER, PAUL AND MARY ★ BOB DYLAN
CHAD MITCHELL TRIO ★ THE WEAVERS
SMOTHERS BROTHERS ★ LIMELITERS ★ BURL IVES
PLUS
MUSIC ARRANGED FOR GUITAR, UKE, BANJO, PIANO, VIOLIN, VOICE
HOUSE OF THE RISING SUN ★ MIDNIGHT SPECIAL
THE FOX ★ PAY ME MY MONEY DOWN
THE ROVING KIND ★ BARBARA ALLEN
LORD RANDALL ★ FOLLOW THE DRINKING GOURD
HUSH, LITTLE BABY ★ DARLING COREY
THIS LAND IS YOUR LAND ★ GREENSLEEVES
SHENANDOAH ★ WE SHALL OVERCOME
WORDS TO HOOT HITS
DANCE the newest craze... "THE HOOT"
M.G.M.'s new movie. ABC's TV show
HOOTENANNY

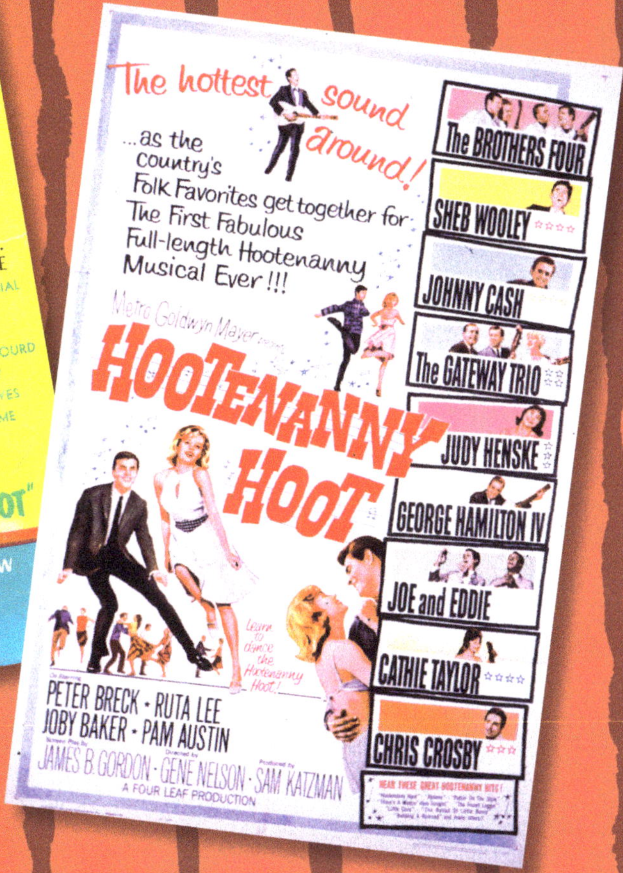
The hottest sound around!
...as the country's Folk Favorites get together for The First Fabulous Full-length Hootenanny Musical Ever!!!
Metro-Goldwyn-Mayer presents
HOOTENANNY HOOT
The BROTHERS FOUR
SHEB WOOLEY
JOHNNY CASH
The GATEWAY TRIO
JUDY HENSKE
GEORGE HAMILTON IV
JOE and EDDIE
CATHIE TAYLOR
CHRIS CROSBY
PETER BRECK · RUTA LEE
JOBY BAKER · PAM AUSTIN
JAMES B. GORDON · GENE NELSON · SAM KATZMAN
A FOUR LEAF PRODUCTION

Tom Rush, concert flyer, Town Hall, January 6, 1967.

MacColl and Seeger, concert flyer, Town Hall, May 1, 1970.

Phil Ochs, concert flyer, Cambridge, MA, November 6, 1965.

Malvina Reynolds et al., concert flyer for Broadside fundraiser, Berkeley, CA, April 13, 1963.

The Friends of Old Time Music, concert flyer, New York, May 2, 1964.

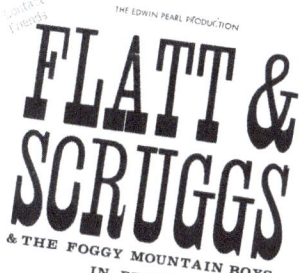
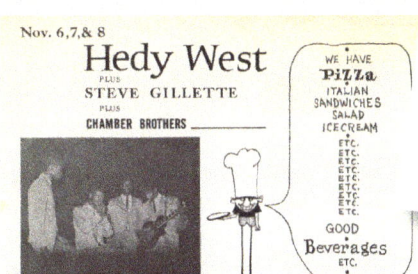

Clarence Ashley, concert flyer, New York, March 25, 1961.

WBAI Club & Broadside, concert flyer, New York, March 8, 1963.

Ash Grove, concert flyer, Los Angeles, 1960s.

Freedom Singers, concert program, New York, Feb. 26, 1963.

Flatt & Scruggs, concert flyer, Berkeley, CA, June 16, 1962.

Hedy West and Theodore Bikel, concert notices, Southern California.

120

Joan Baez on cover of *Time*, November 23, 1962.

Carolyn Hester on cover of the *Saturday Evening Post*, May 30, 1964.

Bob Dylan on cover of the *Saturday Evening Post*, November 2, 1968.

Judy Collins on cover of *Life*, May 2, 1969.

Peter, Paul and Mary on cover of *Cosmopolitan*, December 1963.

Oscar Brand and Judy Collins on cover of *Liberty*, February 19, 1964, a Canadian publication.

Lennon Sisters on cover of *TV, Radio, Movie Reporter*, vol. 1, no. 4 (March 1964).

Odetta: Recorded Folk Songs (New York: M. Witmark & Sons, 1963).

The Village Stompers at Washington Square (New York: Rayven Music Co., 1963).

Broadside! August 1963, published in Los Angeles.

Folk Music, August 1964.

Folk Today! (New York: M. Witmark & Sons, 1965).

Josh Dunson, *Freedom in the Air: Song Movements of the Sixties* (New York: International Publishers, 1965).

Robert Shelton and Burt Goldblatt, *The Country Music Story* (Seacaucus, NJ: Castle Books, 1966).

Woody Guthrie, *Born to Win*, ed. Robert Shelton (New York: Macmillan Co., 1965).

Joan Baez on cover of *Good News*, April 1962, published in Los Angeles.

Joan Baez, souvenir program, 1965.

The Joan Baez Songbook (New York: Ryerson Music Pub., 1964).

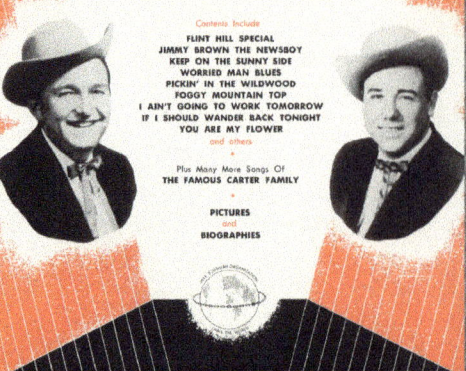

The Weavers' Song Book (New York: Harper & Row, Pub., 1960).

Walt Disney's Ballad of Davy Crockett: Hootenanny Song Album (Miami Beach, FL: Hansen Publications, Inc., 1963).

Norman Luboff and Win Stracke, *Songs of Man* (Englewood Cliffs, NJ: Prentice-Hall, Inc., 1965).

Jay Edwards and Robert Kelley, *The Coffee House Songbook* (New York: Oak Publications, 1966).

Lester Flatt & Earl Scruggs with the Foggy Mountain Boys (New York: Peer International Corp., 1962).

The No. 1 Folk Song Album (New York: Hollis Music, Inc., ca. 1963).

104 Folk Songs as Recorded on Folkways Records by Famous Folk Song Singers (New York: Robbins Music Corp., 1964).

The Bob Gibson Song Book (New York: TRO, 1965).

Young Folk Song Book (New York: Simon and Schuster, 1963).

The Mitchell Trio Song Book (Chicago: Quadrangle Books, 1964).

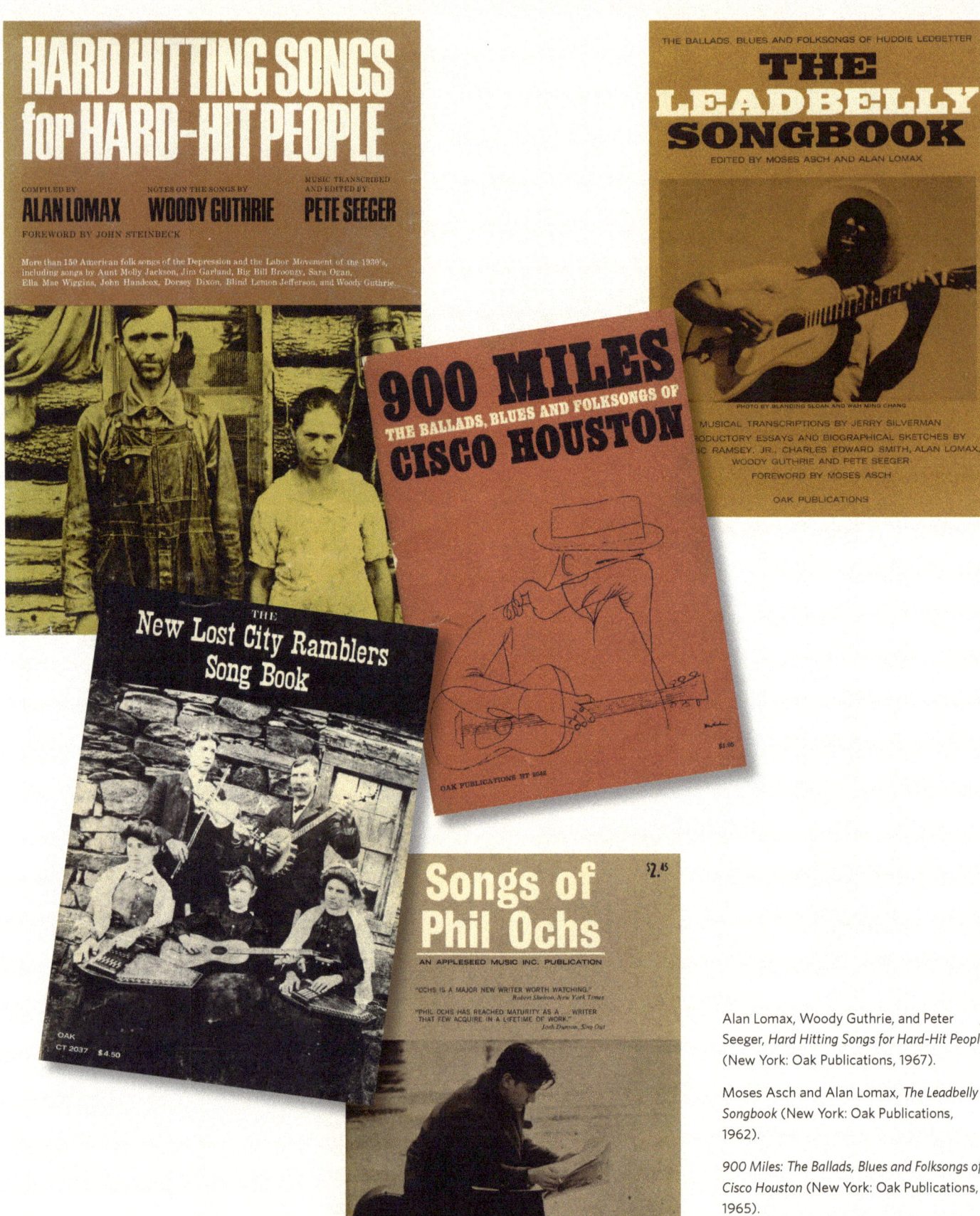

Alan Lomax, Woody Guthrie, and Peter Seeger, *Hard Hitting Songs for Hard-Hit People* (New York: Oak Publications, 1967).

Moses Asch and Alan Lomax, *The Leadbelly Songbook* (New York: Oak Publications, 1962).

900 Miles: The Ballads, Blues and Folksongs of Cisco Houston (New York: Oak Publications, 1965).

The New Lost City Ramblers Song Book (New York: Oak Publications, 1964).

Songs of Phil Ochs (New York: Appleseed Music, Inc., 1964).

Jean Thomas, *Ballad Makin' in the Mountains of Kentucky* (New York: Henry Holt Co., 1939; reprinted, New York: Oak Publications, 1964).

Folk Songs of Peggy Seeger (New York: Oak Publications, 1964).

The Bells of Rhymney and Other Songs and Stories from the Singing of Pete Seeger (New York: Oak Publications, 1964).

Ramblin' Boy and Other Songs by Tom Paxton (New York: Oak Publications, 1964).

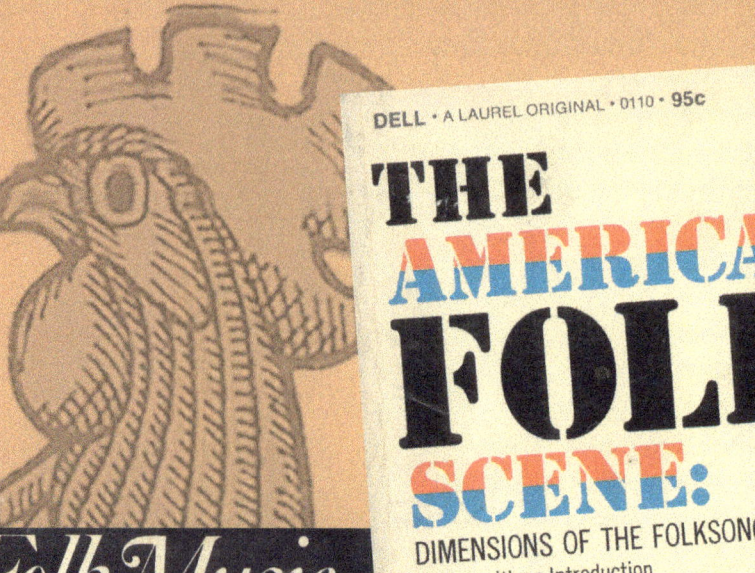

David Gahr and Robert Shelton, *The Face of Folk Music* (New York: Citadel Press, 1968).

David A. DeTurk and A. Poulin, Jr., eds., *The American Folk Scene: Dimensions of the Folksong Revival* (New York: Dell Pub. Co., 1967).

The Newport Folk Festival Songbook (New York: Alfred Music Co., 1965).

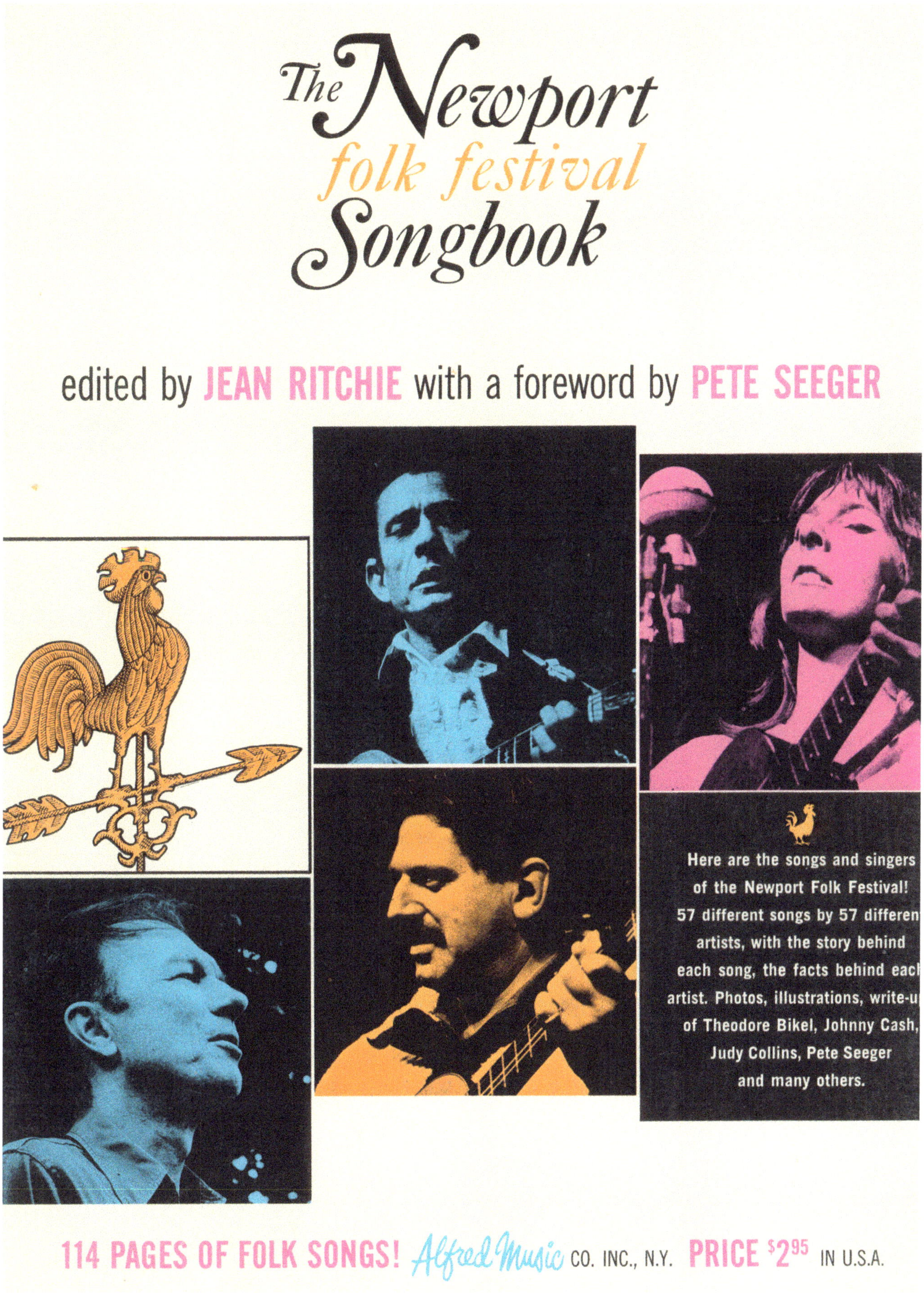
The Newport
folk festival
Songbook
edited by JEAN RITCHIE with a foreword by PETE SEEGER
Here are the songs and singers of the Newport Folk Festival! 57 different songs by 57 differen artists, with the story behind each song, the facts behind eac artist. Photos, illustrations, write-u of Theodore Bikel, Johnny Cash, Judy Collins, Pete Seeger and many others.
114 PAGES OF FOLK SONGS! Alfred Music CO. INC., N.Y. PRICE $2.95 IN U.S.A.

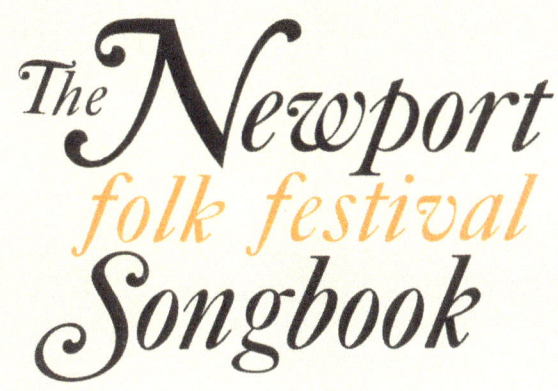

Sir Lancelot, "Walk in Peace," poster, Charter Records, 110.

"People for Peace Concert," Boston, May 4, 1965, sponsored by Students for a Democratic Society.

"Sing-In for Peace," Carnegie Hall, concert flyer, September 24, 1965.

Songs for Peace

Compiled and edited by The Student Peace Union
Introduction by Pete Seeger

OAK PUBLICATIONS $2.95

The Muse of Parker Street

More Songs
by Malvina Reynolds

ORIGINAL ILLUSTRATIONS BY JODI ROBBIN

OAK PUBLICATIONS $2.45

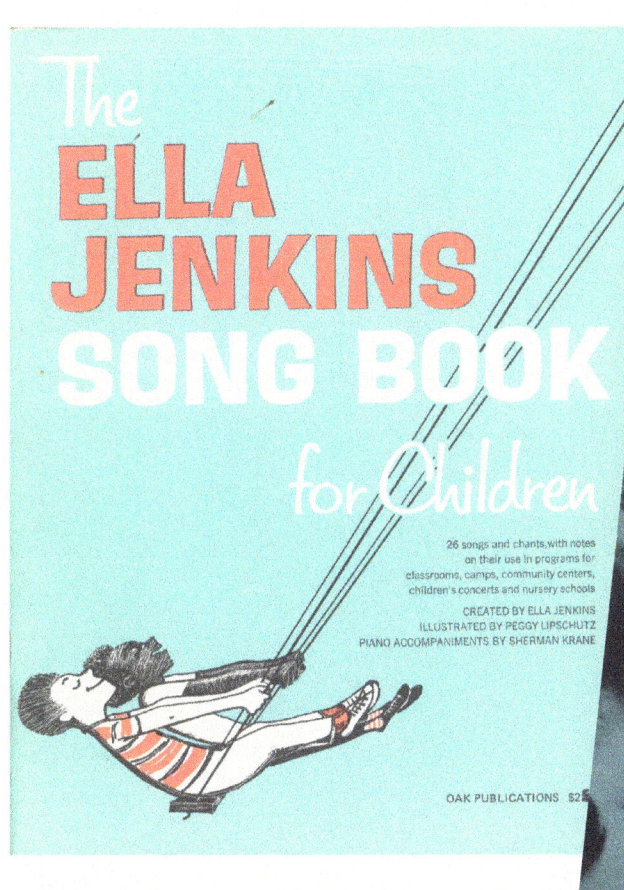

The Student Peace Union, *Songs for Peace* (New York: Oak Publications, 1966).

Ewan MacColl Peggy Seeger Songbook (New York: Oak Publications, 1963).

The Muse of Parker Street: More Songs by Malvina Reynolds (New York: Oak Publications, 1967).

Eric von Schmidt, *Come for to Sing* (Boston: Houghton Mifflin Co., 1963).

The Ella Jenkins Song Book for Children (New York: Oak Publications, 1966).

Guy and Candie Carawan, *We Shall Overcome: Songs of the Southern Freedom Movement* (New York: Oak Publications, 1963).

American Favorite Ballads: Tunes and Songs as Sung by Pete Seeger (New York: Oak Publications, 1961).

Sing Out! vol. 15, no. 4, September 1965.

Rag Baby, vol. 1, no. 2, October 1965, published in Berkeley.

Tune Up, vol. 2, no. 2, December 1963, published in Philadelphia.

Sing Out! vol. 16, no. 1, February–March 1966.

Hit Parader, December 1963.

"Folk Rock Is a Drag," advertisement for Hagstrom Guitars, featuring Frank Zappa.

Song Hits Magazine, vol. 28, no. 4, January 1964.

Rock Folk Song Folio, no. 1, Spring 1966.

Rock Folk Song Folio, no. 2, Summer 1966.

Rock Folk Song Folio, no. 3, Fall 1966.

Rock Folk Song Folio, no. 4, Winter 1966–1967.

Rock Folk Songs, Winter 1965.

Bob Dylan, *The Times They Are a-Changin'* (New York: M. Witmark & Sons, 1963).

Bob Dylan, "Mr. Tambourine Man," sheet music, 1964.

John Denver, "Leaving on a Jet Plane," sheet music, 1967.

Woody Guthrie, "This Land Is Your Land," sheet music, ca. 1964, Canadian adaptation.

Malvina Reynolds, "What Have They Done to the Rain?" sheet music, 1964.

The Rooftop Singers, "Tom Cat," sheet music, 1963.

Dave Fisher, "Cotton Fields," sheet music, 1961.

P. F. Sloan, "Eve of Destruction," sheet music, 1965.

Leo Maguire, "The Gypsy Rover," sheet music, 1962.

Malvina Reynolds, "Little Boxes," sheet music, 1964.

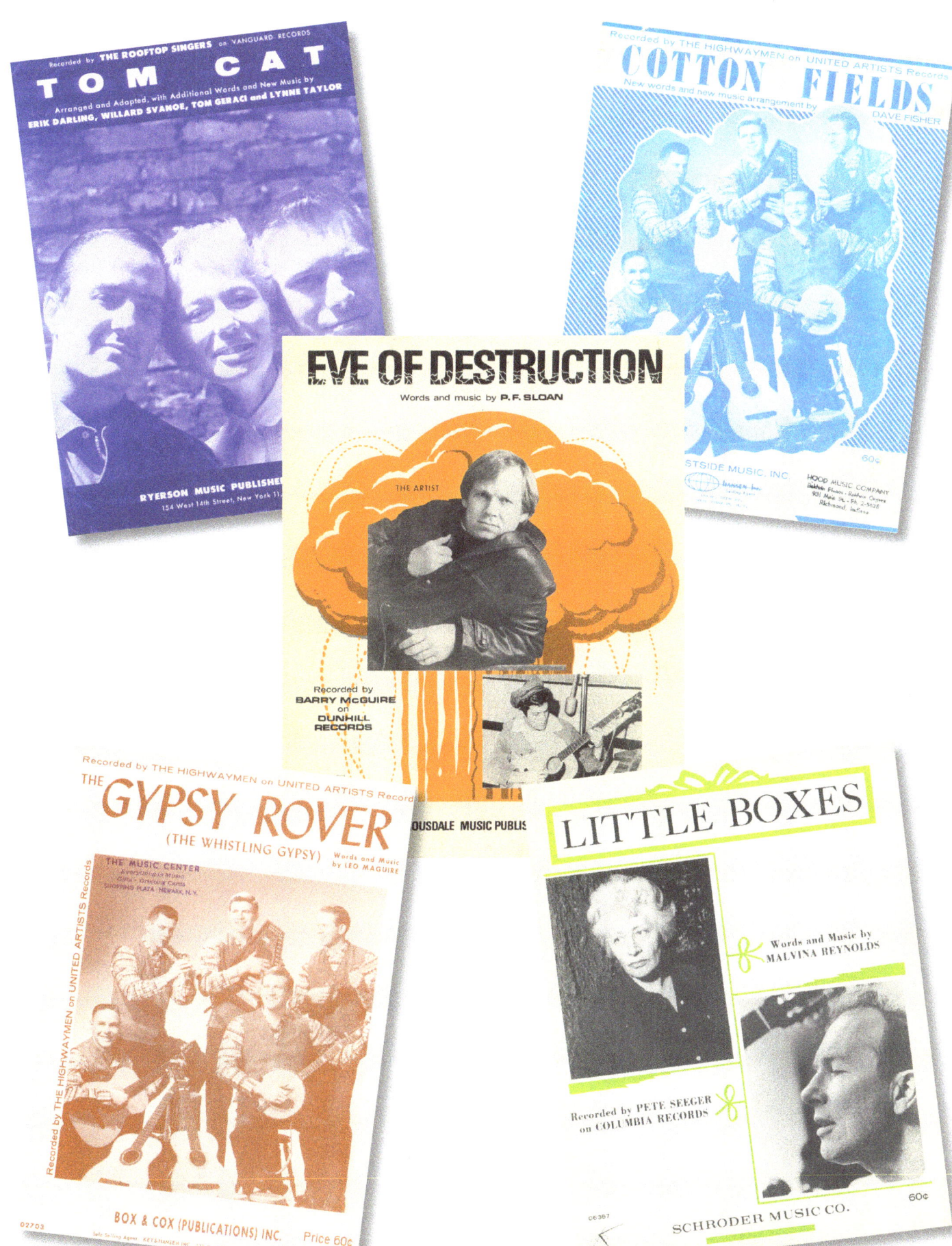

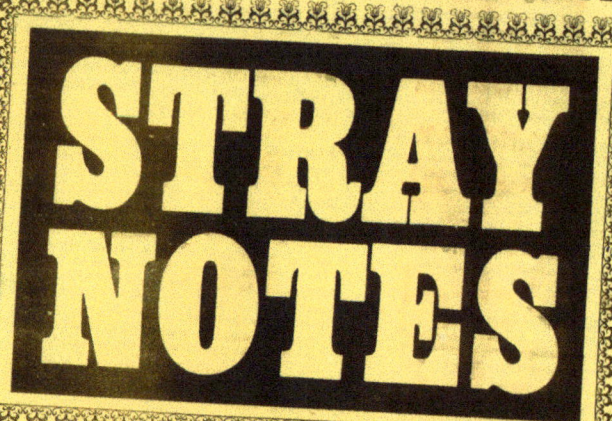

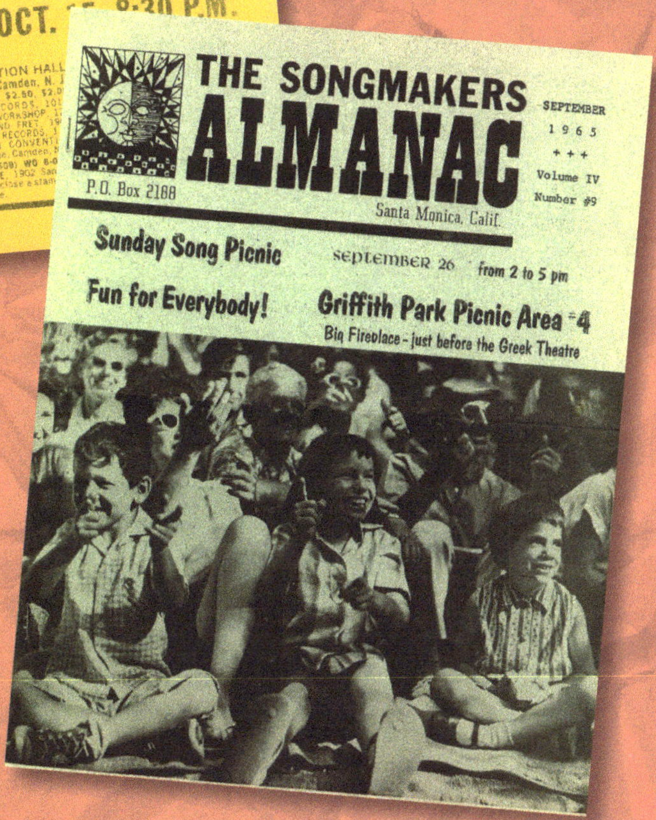

The Folk Scene, vol. 1, no. 1, May 29, 1964, published in Aurora, Illinois, for Chicago area.

The Atlanta Folk Music Society, *Stray Notes*, vol. 1, no. 1, June 1, 1965.

Schedule for the 2nd Fret, Philadelphia, Fall 1965.

The Songmakers Almanac, vol. 4, no. 9, September 1965, published in Los Angeles.

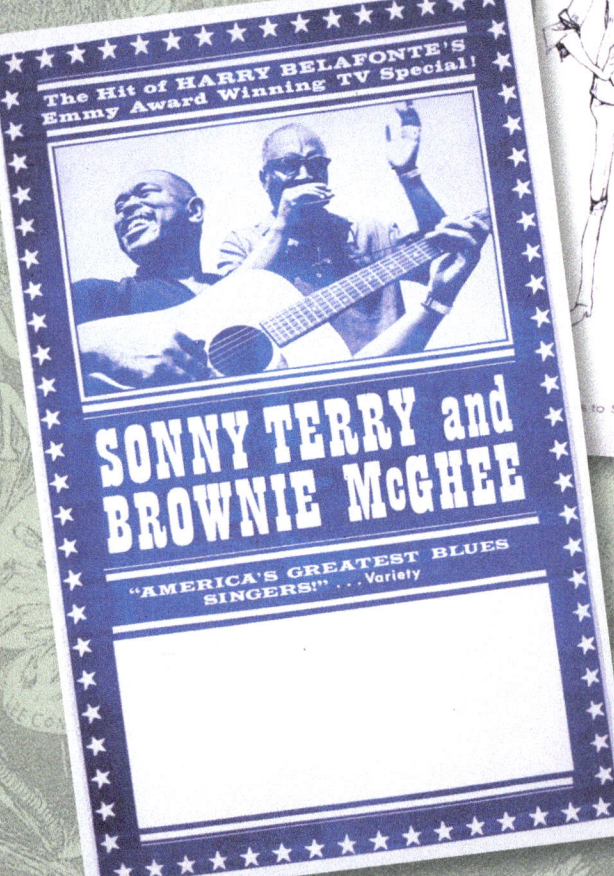

Joan Baez, flyer, ca. 1967.

Joan Baez peace concert, flyer, October 8, 1966.

Pete Seeger, concert flyer, October 19, 1966.

Sonny Terry and Brownie McGhee, concert flyer, ca. 1966.

Sonny Terry and Brownie McGhee at the Fillmore and Winterland, postcard, 1967.

Arlo Guthrie, concert flyer, Masonic Temple, San Francisco, May 18, 1968.

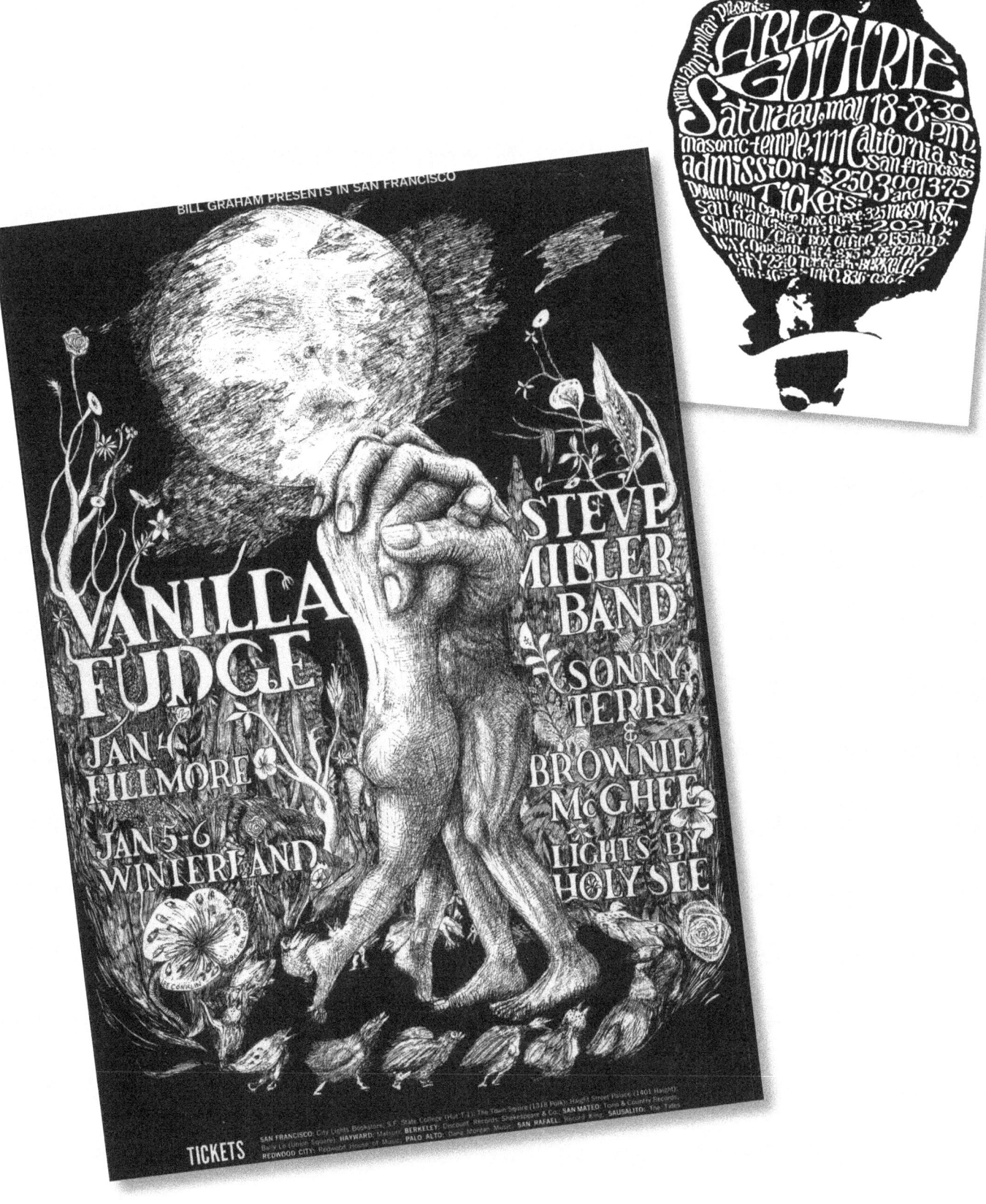

Newport Folk Festival, program, July 21–24, 1966.

Newport Folk Festival, program, July 23–26, 1964.

San Diego Folk Festival, program, May 11–13, 1967.

Philadelphia Folk Festival, program, 1965.

UCLA Folk Music Festival, program, May 3–5, 1963.

Newport Folk Festival, program, July 10–16, 1967.

Philadelphia Folk Festival, program, 1967.

Philadelphia Folk Festival, program, 1966.

Tenth Annual Berkeley Folk Music Festival, program, June 30–July 4, 1967.

Berkeley Folk Music Festival, flyer, June 30–July 4, 1966.

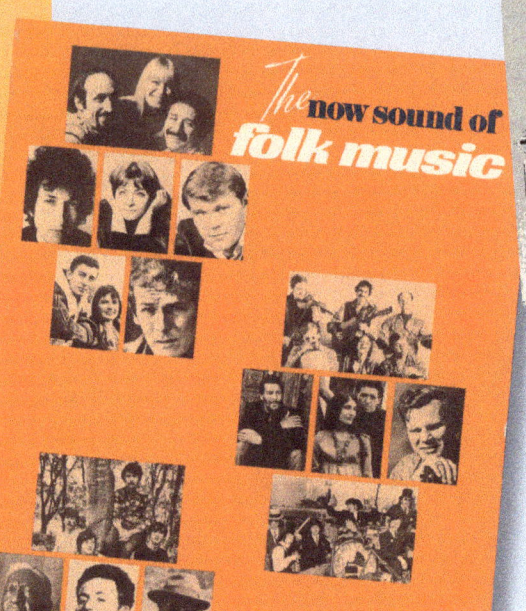

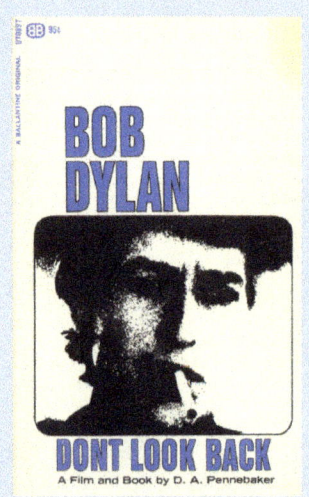

Country Joe and the Fish, concert poster, Avalon Ballroom, San Francisco, 1967.

10th Annual Berkeley Folk Music Festival, program, June 30–July 4, 1967.

The Now Sound of Folk Music (np: Warner Bros.–Seven Arts, Inc., 1967).

Dont Look Back, movie poster (Leacock-Pennebaker, 1967).

D. A. Pennebaker, *Bob Dylan: Dont Look Back* (New York: Ballantine Books, 1968).

Folk Forum, vol. 1, no. 10, September–October 1969, published in Baltimore.

Folk Artists '69, magazine covering the 1969 Newport Folk Festival (Providence, RI: C. Nigro Pub. Co., 1969).

Pop Folk (Los Angeles: West Coast Publications, 1971).

Festival, movie poster (Peppercorn-Wormser, 1967).

Pete Seeger On Record (New York: TRO, 1970).

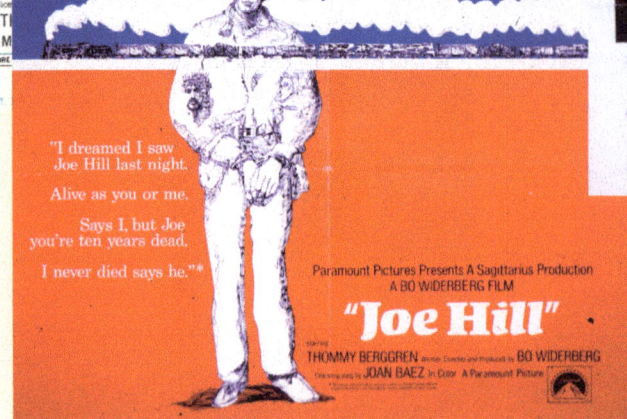

Pressbook for *Celebration at Big Sur*, 20th Century Fox, 1971.

Celebration at Big Sur, movie poster, 20th Century Fox, 1971; film of 1969 Big Sur Folk Festival.

Leadbelly, movie poster, Paramount, 1976.

Arlo Guthrie, "Alice's Restaurant," sheet music, 1969.

Bound for Glory, movie poster, United Artists, 1976.

Joe Hill, movie poster, Paramount, 1971.

Newport Folk Festival, program, July 16–18, 1971 (festival canceled).

Alan Lomax cartoon, *Punch*, July 24, 1957 (British publication).

NOTES ON ILLUSTRATIONS

14: Sheet music and songbooks, while published earlier, began proliferating after the Civil War, and by the early twentieth century were very common throughout the country. Some included songs collected by professional collectors, such as the Englishman Cecil Sharp (1859–1924), who traveled around the South in the second decade of the century. For an introduction to the general topic, see Ronald D. Cohen, *Folk Music: The Basics* (New York: Routledge, 2006).

15: Labor unions and radical movements, such as the Industrial Workers of the World (IWW), published songbooks and sheet music in the twentieth century. There were also books of older African American songs, such as spirituals, first published in the nineteenth century and common by the 1920s. See Ronald D. Cohen, *Work and Sing: A History of Occupational and Labor Unions Songs in the United States* (Crockett, CA: Carquinez Press, 2010).

16: Carl Sandburg (1878–1967), the famed poet, author, and speaker, published the first comprehensive book of folk songs, drawn from his travels as well as published collections. Sandburg included both urban and rural songs from throughout the country.

17: By the 1920s, record companies, such as Victor, began releasing recordings by southern rural performers, black and white. Moreover, songbooks and sheet music continued to flood the market, including songs centering on hobos. Many homes included pianos and guitars, with homegrown performing being common. See Barry Mazor, *Ralph Peer and the Making of Popular Roots Music* (Chicago: Chicago Review Press, 2014); and Ben Wynne, *In Tune: Charley Patton, Jimmie Rodgers, and the Roots of American Music* (Baton Rouge: Louisiana State University Press, 2014).

18: Cowboy and western singers had become popular by the 1930s, particularly Gene Autry (1907–1998), the most popular of the singing movie cowboys, followed by Tom Mix (1880–1940) and numerous others. See Douglas B. Green, *Singing in the Saddle: The History of the Singing Cowboy* (Nashville: Vanderbilt University Press, 2002).

19: In 1910, John Lomax (1867–1948) became the first to publish a scholarly book on cowboy songs, followed, in 1931, by Margaret Larkin (1899–1967). They established cowboy and western songs as part of the country's folk music legacy. See Nolan Porterfield, *Last Cavalier: The Life and Times of John Lomax, 1867–1948* (Urbana: University of Illinois Press, 1996).

20: Folk music included various musical styles and lyrics by the 1930s. The *Workers Song Book* included mostly songs by modernist composers with little connection to the country's working class. See Richard A. Reuss and JoAnne C. Reuss, *American Folk Music and Left-Wing Politics, 1927–1957* (Lanham, MD: Scarecrow Press, 2000).

21: Huddie Ledbetter, better known as Lead Belly (1888–1949), was released from a southern prison in 1934 after being discovered by John and Alan Lomax. He would become one of the most influential of the country's singer-songwriters. See Charles Wolfe and

Kip Lornell, *The Life and Legend of Leadbelly* (New York: HarperCollins, 1992).

22: By the 1940s, Paul Robeson (1898–1967) had become a world-famous singer, actor, and political activist. He performed many African American and radical songs. The White Top Folk Festival in Virginia, as was common among southern folk festivals of the time, did not include black performers. See Sheila Tully Boyle and Andrew Bunie, *Paul Robeson: The Years of Promise and Achievement* (Amherst: University of Massachusetts Press, 2001); Martin Duberman, *Paul Robeson* (New York: Knopf, 1988); and Ronald D. Cohen, *A History of Folk Music Festivals in the United States* (Lanham, MD: Scarecrow Press, 2008).

23: John and Alan Lomax (1915–2002) published this book of Lead Belly's songs in 1936. See John Szwed, *Alan Lomax: The Man Who Recorded the World* (New York: Viking Books, 2010).

24: Lawrence Gellert (1898–1979?) collected African American songs in the South beginning in the 1920s. Many have been considered protest songs and were first published by the American Music League, connected to the Communist Party, although this interpretation has been questioned by Bruce Conforth in *African American Folksong and American Cultural Politics: The Lawrence Gellert Story* (Lanham, MD: Scarecrow Press, 2013). The Lomaxes followed Sandburg in publishing an influential book of folksongs, drawn from their own southern collecting trips.

25: This colorful sheet music included three songs collected by John Lomax, arranged by the composer of western songs, Oscar Fox (1879–1961), while Melvin LeMon published this book of mining songs.

26–27: Song folios—paperbound books of songs and also including music—of hillbilly ballads were popular by the 1930s. John Jacob Niles (1892–1980) collected and performed southern songs in a rather formal style. See Ron Pen, *I Wonder as I Wander: The Life of John Jacob Niles* (Lexington: University Press of Kentucky, 2010).

28–29: In the 1930s, radical and labor songbooks were published by various left-wing organizations, such as the Socialist Party, through the Rand School Press, as well as various labor unions, including the Textile Workers Union.

30–31: There were numerous cowboy song folios published in the 1930s, when singing cowboys were common in Hollywood films and on radio programs.

32–33: Lead Belly recorded a number of 78 rpm albums in the 1930s and '40s, as did the African American musician Josh White (1914–1969), who became one of the most popular folk performers by the '40s. See Elijah Wald, *Josh White: Society Blues* (Amherst: University of Massachusetts Press, 2000).

34: Many political radicals in the late 1930s supported the Abraham Lincoln Brigade, made up of US volunteers who traveled to Spain after 1936 to fight for the government against the army and other fascist insurgents in the civil war. The opposition was backed by the German Nazi government and the Italian fascist military, while the US remained neutral until the Spanish government surrendered in 1939. Music became very important in supporting the socialist government, and this album in 1943 included Pete Seeger, Tom Glazer, Baldwin Hawes, and Bess Hawes.

35: By the 1960s, Woody Guthrie (1912–1967) had become one of the most influential singer-songwriters. Along with Josh White, Lead Belly, and Pete Seeger, Guthrie was part of the broad folk music revival that also included country and blues musicians. See Ronald D. Cohen, *Woody Guthrie: Writing America's Music* (New York: Routledge, 2012); and Will Kaufman, *Woody Guthrie: American Radical* (Urbana: University of Illinois Press, 2011).

36–37: Pete Seeger (1919–2014), Lee Hays (1914–1981), and Millard Lampell (1919–1997) started the Almanac Singers in New York City in 1941. They were joined by others, including Woody Guthrie, to promote what was initially a singing labor and peace movement; they disbanded in 1943. Guthrie published his fictionalized autobiography, *Bound for Glory*, in 1943, and later joined others in the Folkways Records album *Lonesome Valley*. See David King Dunaway, *How Can I Keep from Singing? The Ballad of Pete Seeger* (New York: Villard, 2008).

38–39: Race (black) and hillbilly (white) recordings continued through the 1940s, when Burl Ives

(1909–1995) began his popular career as a musician and actor. Moses Asch (1905–1986) launched his various labels during World War II, including the influential Folkways Records after 1949. He issued thousands of albums, now controlled by Smithsonian-Folkways. See Richard Carlin, *Worlds of Sound: The Story of Smithsonian Folkways* (New York: Smithsonian, 2008); and Peter Goldsmith, *Making People's Music: Moe Asch and Folkways Records* (Washington, DC: Smithsonian, 1998).

40–41: Jack Guthrie, Woody's cousin, had a hit with Woody's "Oklahoma Hills" in 1946. Through the decade, Josh White, Burl Ives, and John Jacob Niles kept folk music before the general public.

42–43: Folk music continued to take various musical forms during World War II, including work and international songs, as shown by these very different published song collections.

44–45: Pete Seeger began his musical career before the war, joining Paul Robeson and others in connecting folk music with a radical political agenda. See Ronald D. Cohen and James Capaldi, eds., *The Pete Seeger Reader* (New York: Oxford University Press, 2014).

46–47: While the elderly John Lomax published his memoir and the much-younger Burl Ives his autobiography following the war, numerous songbooks became increasingly popular.

48–49: Pete Seeger, Woody Guthrie, and their musical friends launched People's Songs in early 1946 to stimulate a folk song movement that supported civil rights, labor unions, and international cooperation. The organization, along with its informative bulletin, lasted into early 1949. They battled the escalating Cold War and internal political repression of the Left. See Robbie Lieberman, *"My Song Is My Weapon": People's Songs, American Communism, and the Politics of Culture, 1930–1950* (Urbana: University of Illinois Press, 1989).

50–51: Tom Glazer (1914–2003) was a musician and prolific composer who participated in numerous progressive concerts. People's Songs issued two small, plastic records promoting Henry Wallace's presidential campaign on the Progressive Party's ticket in 1948. Wallace came in fourth, with the Democrat Harry Truman emerging as the winner.

52–53: *The Fireside Book of Folk Songs* quickly became very popular, while Richard Dyer-Bennet (1913–1991) joined John Jacob Niles in presenting folk music in a formal concert setting. See Paul Jenkins, *Richard Dyer-Bennet: The Last Minstrel* (Jackson: University Press of Mississippi, 2009).

54–55: Folk songs had long appealed to children, as indicated by these songbooks by Ruth Crawford Seeger, Pete's stepmother, and Beatrice Landeck. Young People's Records, formed just after the war, issued hundreds of mail-order records, including both classical and folk arrangements, to educate children musically. See David Bonner, *Revolutionizing Children's Records: The Young People's Records and Children's Record Guild Series, 1946–1977* (Lanham, MD: Scarecrow Press, 2007).

56: The Weavers, a quartet consisting of Pete Seeger, Lee Hays, Ronnie Gilbert, and Fred Hellerman, had a major hit in 1950 with "Goodnight, Irene," which was soon recorded by many others, including Frank Sinatra. This launched a fresh folk music revival. See Ronald D. Cohen and Rachel C. Donaldson, *Roots of the Revival: American and British Folk Music in the 1950s* (Urbana: University of Illinois Press, 2014).

57: In 1952, Folkways Records issued this six record set of prewar race and hillbilly recordings compiled by the collector Harry Smith (1923–1991). It would become influential in introducing a new audience to this southern folk-style music. In 1950, with the demise of People's Songs and its bulletin, *Sing Out!* magazine emerged to promote folk music and left-wing politics. This 1959 issue featured Alan Lomax, who had recently returned to New York after eight years in Great Britain.

58: In the 1950s, partly because of the popularity of the Weavers, until they were blacklisted by 1953, folk music was becoming part of popular music, as this sheet music indicates. See Rachel Clare Donaldson, *"I Hear America Singing": Folk Music and National Identity* (Philadelphia: Temple University Press, 2014).

59: *Sing Out!* promoted a singing interracial movement through its articles and concerts. Irwin Silber

(1925–2010) remained as editor until the late 1960s.

60–61: The Weavers would become influential in stimulating subsequent folk groups, including the Limeliters, the Gateway Singers, and particularly the Kingston Trio (Dave Guard, Bob Shane, and Nick Reynolds), who had a major hit with "Tom Dooley" in 1958, soon followed by many others. See William J. Bush, *Greenback Dollar: The Incredible Rise of the Kingston Trio* (Lanham, MD: Scarecrow Press, 2013).

62–63: Pete Seeger, along with the Weavers, heavily promoted folk music through the decade. See Ronald D. Cohen, *Rainbow Quest: The Folk Music Revival and American Society, 1940–1970* (Amherst: University of Massachusetts Press, 2002).

64: The 1950 anti-communist publication *Red Channels* listed many folk performers (along with actors and dozens of others), including Pete Seeger, which stimulated their blacklisting.

65: The folklorist D. K. Wilgus's important study, *Anglo-American Folksong Scholarship Since 1898* (New Brunswick: Rutgers University Press, 1959), helped document the recent history of this growing academic field. Meanwhile Harry Belafonte (b. 1927) had become a very popular singer, in particular popularizing calypso-style songs. Magazines such as *16* and *Teen*, appealing to the growing youth market, featured Belafonte for a brief time during the middle of the decade. See Judith Smith, *Becoming Belafonte: Black Artist, Public Radical* (Austin, TX: University of Texas Press, 2014).

66–67: The Weavers, Guy Carawan, Bob Gibson, and Belafonte were some of the performers promoting folk music in the 1950s. While Woody Guthrie was confined to a hospital because of his crippling Huntington's disease, many performers headlined a concert in his honor in 1958.

68–69: Sea songs had long been part of folk music, along with other styles appearing in such songbooks as Carl Sandburg's 1950 addition to his popular *American Songbag*.

70–71: Malvina Reynolds (1900–1978) emerged as a prolific singer-songwriter, while Brownie McGhee (1915–1996) continued as an influential blues performer. Frank Warner (1903–1978) became an active ballad collector and performer.

72–73: While Belafonte popularized "Day-O" as a calypso standard, it was also performed under the title "The Banana Boat Song" by the Tarriers, a trio that included the actor Alan Arkin and the talented musician Erik Darling (1933–2008).

74–77: Calypso's popularity was brief, featuring recordings by the Tarriers, the Easy Riders, and particularly Belafonte.

78–79: By the late 1950s, various trios and quartets were emerging, including the Shanty Boys and the Greenbriar Boys playing bluegrass music in New York. *Caravan*, *Gardyloo*, and *The Little Sandy Review* were folk magazines that emerged to spread the word.

80–81: Folk music was part of the do-it-yourself movement of the 1950s, including learning to play the acoustic guitar and banjo. Pete Seeger first published his influential banjo instruction book in 1948, while Vega produced a "Seeger Model" 5-string long-neck banjo in 1960.

82–83: Jac Holzman (b. 1931) founded Elektra Records in 1950, and issued this kit in 1959. Israel G. "Izzy" Young (b. 1928) opened his influential Folklore Center in Greenwich Village in 1957, although he had been selling folklore books for a few years before then. His "Frets and Frails" column in *Sing Out!* connected folk fans throughout the country. See Scott Barretta, ed., *The Conscience of the Folk Revival: The Writings of Israel "Izzy" Young* (Lanham, MD: Scarecrow Press, 2013).

84–85: Folk festivals were not new, but the Newport Folk Festival, beginning in 1959, would become the most influential, while the Berkeley Folk Festival would join other emerging college festivals. Meanwhile, folk music concerts proliferated in New York City. See Ronald D. Cohen, *A History of Folk Music Festivals in the United States* (Lanham, MD: Scarecrow Press, 2008).

86–87: The popularity of the Kingston Trio led to the emergence of numerous other groups, including the Highwaymen and the Journeymen.

88–89: Folk clubs, such as the Ash Grove in Los Angeles, proliferated in the late 1950s and into the '60s. Skiffle music, based on American blues, country, and jazz, briefly emerged in England as a popular style in the mid-1950s.

90–91: These notices included many who had become rising performers by the late 1950s. Gerde's Folk City in Greenwich Village emerged as the most influential of the local establishments in the early 1960s. See Ian Zack, *Say No to the Devil: The Life and Musical Genius of Rev. Gary Davis* (Chicago: University of Chicago Press, 2015).

92–93: A few feature films focused on folk music, while some included calypso musicians.

94–95: Folksong books also proliferated as inexpensive paperbacks, feeding into the popularity of folk singing by the early 1960s.

96–97: John Cohen, Ralph Rinzler, and Izzy Young formed the Friends of Old Time Music in 1961 to promote older country and blues musicians in New York concerts, sometimes joined by the New Lost City Ramblers. Judy Collins (b. 1939) began her stellar career in Colorado. See Ray Allen, *Gone to the Country: The New Lost City Ramblers and the Folk Music Revival* (Urbana: University of Illinois Press, 2010); Judy Collins, *Sweet Judy Blue Eyes: My Life in Music* (New York: Thorndike Press, 2012); and Stephen Petrus and Ronald D. Cohen, *Folk City: New York and the American Folk Music Revival* (New York: Oxford University Press, 2015).

98–99: Bob Dylan (born Robert Zimmerman, 1941) arrived in Greenwich Village in 1961 and quickly made a name for himself, leading to his appearance on the cover of *Sing Out!* in 1963. He soon joined the Kingston Trio and Peter, Paul and Mary in popularizing folk music, as indicated in this 1962 *Gordo* comic strip. See Dennis McDougal, *Dylan: The Biography* (New York: Turner Publishing Co., 2014); and David Hajdu, *Positively 4th Street: The Lives and Times of Joan Baez, Bob Dylan, Mimi Baez Fariña and Richard Fariña* (New York: Farrar, Straus and Giroux, 2001).

100–101: By the mid-1960s, folk music was popular throughout the country. Dave Van Ronk (1936–2002), a mainstay of the Greenwich Village folk scene, appeared in a concert in 1964 at Indiana University, as did the traditional performer Doc Watson (1923–2012) in 1965. The Weavers continued into the early 1960s, as did the blues performer Barbara Dane and so many others. See Dave Van Ronk with Elijah Wald, *The Mayor of MacDougal Street: A Memoir* (Cambridge, MA: DaCapo Press, 2005).

102–3: While Woody Guthrie languished in a hospital until his death in 1967, his songs were becoming increasingly familiar to listeners. The Lee Hays-Pete Seeger composition "If I Had a Hammer" was popularized by Peter, Paul and Mary, as well as Trini Lopez.

104–5: Sis Cunningham (1909–2004) and her husband, Gordon Friesen (1909–1996), launched *Broadside*, a topical songs magazine, in 1962. It quickly featured Bob Dylan, Malvina Reynolds, Pete Seeger, Phil Ochs, and many other singer-songwriters until its demise in the 1980s. Izzy Young featured Dylan in his first concert hall appearance in November 1961. The Newport Folk Festival opened in 1959 for two years, then reopened in 1963 and lasted until the end of the decade.

106–7: By mid-decade, a wide variety of performance styles were popular in festivals and concerts, including bluegrass, protest music, blues and gospel, and songs from singer-songwriters.

108–11: In 1963 and 1964, the term "hootenanny," first discovered by Woody Guthrie and Pete Seeger in 1941, shorthand for a folk music concert, became widespread to sell a variety of products, such as a candy bar, pinball machine, paper dolls, songbooks, record albums, and even comic books. By 1965, it had pretty much faded from usage.

112–13: As "hootenanny" flooded the market, it became the title of a feature film, as well as a few popular magazines.

114–17: Here are more indications of the widespread use of "hootenanny" in commercial products.

118–19: Folk performers, some with a left-wing political agenda, such as Phil Ochs, Malvina Reynolds, Ewan MacColl and Peggy Seeger, and the Freedom Singers, were popular through the decade. Others, such as Clarence Ashley and Flatt and Scruggs, performed traditional country music or bluegrass.

120–21: Popular magazines, such as *Time*, *Life*, and *Cosmopolitan*, featured folk performers, including Joan Baez, Judy Collins, and Bob Dylan.

122–27: Numerous magazines, including the briefly published *Folk Music*, along with books such as Josh Dunson's *Freedom in the Air*, which documented the rise of protest songs, were widespread by mid-decade.

128–29: Oak Publications, owed by Moses Asch and Irwin Silber, published dozens of folk books, including *Hard Hitting Songs for Hard-Hit People*, first compiled by Woody Guthrie, Alan Lomax, and Pete Seeger in 1940 but not issued until 1967.

130–31: With photos by David Gahr and text by the *New York Times* music critic Robert Shelton, *The Face of Folk Music* well captured the thriving folk scene of the time.

132–33: As the peace movement accelerated by mid-decade, these two concerts featured some of the prominent activist performers. See Ronald D. Cohen and Will Kaufman, *Singing for Peace: Antiwar Songs in American History* (Boulder, CO: Paradigm, 2015).

134–35: Peace and civil rights songs were only a small part of the range of folk songs by mid-decade.

136–37: Numerous folk magazines continued to appear, such as *Tune Up* from Philadelphia, while Country Joe McDonald published *Rag Baby* in Berkeley, California. The emergence of folk-rock in 1965 led to various publications, part of the rock music explosion of the time.

138–39: Along with songbooks, sheet music spread folk songs to the proliferating amateur market as well as to professional performers.

140–41: Local folk magazines were published in numerous communities; these included *Stray Notes* in Atlanta and *Songmakers Almanac* in Los Angeles.

142–43: The Bay Area featured not only performances by Pete Seeger and Joan Baez, but also Sonny Terry and Brownie McGhee as well as Arlo Guthrie in large concert halls.

144–45: The Newport, Berkeley, and Philadelphia folk festivals lasted through the 1960s, although only the one in Philadelphia continued into the subsequent decades, as did other festivals throughout the country.

146–47: Folk performers continued into and beyond the 1970s, appearing in magazines, festivals, and on records, particularly including Pete Seeger. See Michael Scully, *The Never-Ending Revival: Rounder Records and the Folk Alliance* (Urbana: University of Illinois Press, 2008).

148–49: A few feature films included folk music performers, stories, and songs. The Newport Folk Festival was scheduled to reopen in 1971, having closed in 1969, but was canceled after this program was published. It was finally brought back in 1985.

INDEX

ABC-TV Hootenanny Folk Songs (periodical), 116
ABC-TV Hootenanny Show (periodical), 116
academic interest in folk music, 154
"Advancing Proletaire, The," 14
African American Folksong and American Cultural Politics: The Lawrence Gellert Story, 11
African American songs, 152
Afro-American Folksongs: A Study in Racial and National Music, 14
Al Compas del Calypso, 92
Alan Lomax, Assistant in Charge: The Library of Congress Letters, 1935–1945, 12
Alan Lomax: The Man Who Recorded the World, 10
"Alice's Restaurant" sheet music, 149
"All for Pete!" concert flyer, 90
"All Over This Land" concert flyer, 90
Allan, Lewis, "The House I Live In," 41
Allen, Ray, *Gone to the Country: The New Lost City Ramblers and the Folk Music Revival*, 10, 155
Almanac Singers, 152; *Songs for John Doe*, 37, 45; *Talking Union*, 48
"American Balladry and Folk Song" program, University of California, Berkeley, 1958, 84
American Ballads and Folk Songs, 8
American Favorite Ballads: Tunes and Songs as Sung by Pete Seeger, 135
American Folk Guitar, 80
American Folk Scene: Dimensions of the Folksong Revival, The, 130
American Folk Songs: A Regional Encyclopedia, 12
American Folk Songs for Children, 55
American Folksong, 34

American Hootenanny: Reprints from Sing Out! The Folk Song Magazine, 114
American Music League, 152
American Negro Songs and Spirituals, 20
American People's Festival, concert notice, 45
American Roots Music, 10
American Sea Songs & Chanteys, 68
American Songbag, The, 8, 16, 154
Anglo-American Ballad Study Book, The, 41
Anglo-American Folksong Scholarship since 1898, 12, 64, 154
Anthology of American Folk Music booklet, 57
Archive of American Folk Song, 7–8
Arkin, Alan, 154; "The Banana Boat Song," 72
Arlo Guthrie: The Warner/Reprise Years, 11
"A-Round the Corner," 59
Asbel, Bernie, People's Songs Hootenanny, 45
Asch, Moses, 103, 153; *The Leadbelly Songbook*, 128; as owner of Oak Publications, 156
Ash Grove (folk club), 154; concert flyers, 1963, 107, 119; poster, 89
Ashley, Clarence, 155; concert flyer, 119
Atlanta Folk Music Society, *Stray Notes*, 141
Attaway, William: *Calypso Song Book*, 74; "Day-O," 72
authenticity defined, 9
Autry, Gene, 151; *Famous Cowboy Songs and Mountain Ballads*, 18

Baez, Joan, 156; flyer ca. 1967, 142; *Good News* cover, 125; peace concert flyer, 142; souvenir program, 1965, 125; *Time* magazine cover, 121

Ballad Collectors of North America: How Gathering Folksongs Transformed Academic Thought and American Identity, The, 12
Ballad Makin' in the Mountains of Kentucky, 129
Ballad Mongers, The, 87
ballads defined, 8
Ballads of Sacco & Vanzetti, 103
"Banana Boat Song, The," 72, 154
Barretta, Scott, *The Conscience of the Folk Revival: The Writings of Israel "Izzy" Young*, 11, 154
Barron, Bob, "Cindy, Oh Cindy," 59
Batman comic guest-starring the Hootenanny Hotshots, 110
Beaumont, Daniel, *Preachin' the Blues: The Life and Times of Son House*, 10
Beautiful Music All Around Us: Field Recordings and the American Experience, The, 12
Becoming Belafonte: Black Artist, Public Radical, 154
Beer, Holly, *Singing Out: An Oral History of America's Folk Music Revivals*, 10
Belafonte, Harry, 154; "Day-O," 72, 154; *Downbeat* cover, 72; at the Empire Room, Chicago, 66; "Island in the Sun," 72; at the Riviera Hotel, Las Vegas, 66; *Time* cover, 72
Belafonte, Harry, with Miriam Makeba, Carter Baron Amphitheater program, 1960, 105
Bells of Rhymney and Other Songs and Stories from the Singing of Pete Seeger, The, 129
Berkeley Folk Music Festival, 154, 156; flyer, 1966, 145; Sixth Annual, 1963, 18, 97; Tenth Annual, 1967, 145, 146
Best Loved American Folk Songs, 47
Big Sur Folk Festival, 1969, 149
Bikel, Theodore, concert notice, 119
Bird, Brian, *Skiffle: The Story of Folk Song with a Jazz Beat*, 89
"Blowin' in the Wind" ad in *Billboard*, 104
"Blue Tail Fly, The," 40
bluegrass music, 8, 154, 155
blues, 8, 9
blues musicians, 152
"Bob Gibson Sings Offbeat Folksongs," 66
Bob Gibson Song Book, The, 127
Boni, Margaret, *Fireside Book of Folk Songs*, 53
Bonner, David, *Revolutionizing Children's Records*, 153

Boone County Jamboree: Favorite Songs of the WLW, 34
Botkin, B. A., 8
Bound for Glory, 37
Bound for Glory movie poster, 149
Boyle, Sheila Tully, *Paul Robeson: The Years of Promise and Achievement*, 152
Brand, Oscar: *The Ballad Mongers*, 87; *Bawdy Songs and Backroom Ballads*, 95; *Folk Songs for Fun*, 95; "A Guy Is a Guy," 59; *Liberty* cover, 121; *Oscar Brand's Authentic Hootenanny Song Book*, 108
Brandeis University 2nd Annual Folk Festival, 1964 flyer, 107
Broadside, 122, 155; concert flyer, 119
Broadside, no. 1, 105
broadsides, history, 8
Brown, Jim, *American Roots Music*, 10
Brownie McGhee Blues, 70
Bunie, Andrew, *Paul Robeson: The Years of Promise and Achievement*, 152
Burgess, Lord: "Day-O," 72; "Island in the Sun," 72
Bush, William J., *Greenback Dollar: The Incredible Rise of the Kingston Trio*, 11, 154

Cabale Coffee House calendar, June 1964, 105
Calypso Album, 77
"Calypso Carnival," 75
Calypso Joe, 92
Calypso Song Book, 75
Calypso Song Craze, 77
Calypso Songs, 77
Calypso Stars, 77
Calypso Steel Band Clash concert flyer, 90
Calypso: The Belafonte Story, 77
Calypso-Land, 75
calypsos, 8
calypso-style songs, 154
Campbell, Big Bill, "The Hill-Billy 'Round-Up' Songbook," 26
Capaldi, James, *The Pete Seeger Reader*, 11, 153
Caravan (folk magazine), 154; "Tree of Folk Music" cover, 79
Carawan, Guy, 66, 154
Carawan, Guy and Candie, *We Shall Overcome: Songs of the Southern Freedom Movement*, 135
Carey, Bob, "The Banana Boat Song," 72

Carlin, Richard: *Country Music: The People, Places, and Moments That Shaped the Country Sound*, 12; *Worlds of Sound: The Story of Smithsonian Folkways*, 10, 153

Carter Family concert notice, 24

Celebration at Big Sur: movie poster, 148; pressbook, 149

Charlton Comics Group, *Love Diary*, 111

Cherry, Don, "So Long, It's Been Good to Know Yuh," 59

Cherry Lane Theatre Swapping Song Fair, 84

Chicago Folk: Images of the Sixties Music Scene: The Photographs of Raeburn Flerlage, 11

"Cindy, Oh Cindy," 59

civil rights songs, 153, 156

Coffee House Songbook, The, 126

Cohen, John, 155

Cohen, Norm: *American Folk Songs: A Regional Encyclopedia*, 12; *Ethnic and Border Music: A Regional Exploration*, 12; *Folk Music: A Regional Exploration*, 12

Cohen, Ronald D.: *Alan Lomax, Assistant in Charge: The Library of Congress Letters, 1935–1945*, 12; *Chicago Folk: Images of the Sixties Music Scene: The Photographs of Raeburn Flerlage*, 11; *Folk City: New York and the American Folk Music Revival*, 11, 155; *Folk Music: The Basics*, 10, 151; *A History of Folk Music Festivals in the United States*, 10–11, 152, 154; *The Pete Seeger Reader*, 11, 153; *Rainbow Quest: The Folk Music Revival and American Society, 1940–1970*, 10, 154; *Roots of the Revival: American and British Folk Music in the 1950s*, 11, 153; *Singing for Peace: Antiwar Songs in American History*, 11, 156; *Woody Guthrie: Writing America's Music*, 152; *Work and Sing: A History of Occupational and Labor Songs in the United States*, 11, 151

Collins, Judy, 155; *Liberty* cover, 121; *Life* magazine cover, 121; *Sweet Judy Blue Eyes: My Life in Music*, 155

Colorado Folk Festival, Denver, program, 1960, 97

Coltman, Bob, *Paul Clayton and the Folksong Revival*, 10

Columbia Records Folk Music Catalog, 82

Come for to Sing, 135

"Commies Go After the Kids, The" cartoon, 65

Communist Party, 152

Conforth, Bruce, *African American Folksong and American Cultural Politics: The Lawrence Gellert Story*, 11, 152

Conscience of the Folk Revival: The Writings of Israel "Izzy" Young, The, 11

coon songs, 9

"Cotton Fields" sheet music, 138

Country Joe and the Fish, concert poster, San Francisco, 1967, 146

Country Music Story, The, 124

country songs, 8

Courlander, Harold, *Negro Folk Music U.S.A.*, 87

cowboy singers, 151

cowboy songs, 8, 152

Cowboy Songs, 30

Cowboy Songs as Sung by John White, 30

Cray, Ed, *Songs from the Ash Grove*, 89

Crosby, Bing, 51

Cunningham, Sis, 155

Dane, Barbara, 155; University of California, Berkeley, concert flyer, 101

Darling, Erik, 154; "The Banana Boat Song," 72

Davison, Archibald T., *140 Folk-Songs: Rote Songs for Grades I, II, and III*, 16

"Day-O," 72, 154

Deane, Eddie V., "Hootenanny" sheet music, 112

Dehr, Richard, "Marianne," 59

Dell Book of Great American Folk Songs, The, 95

Denver, John, "Leaving on a Jet Plane" sheet music, 138

DeTurk, David A., *The American Folk Scene: Dimensions of the Folksong Revival*, 130

Disc record catalog, 7

Discovering Folk Music, 12

D'Lugoff, Burt, 59

Dobkin, Alix, 107

Doc Hopkins and His Country Boys, 34

Doerflinger, William, *Shantymen and Shantyboys*, 68

do-it-yourself movement, 154

Donaldson, Rachel Clare, *"I Hear America Singing": Folk Music and National Identity*, 153

Dont Look Back movie poster, 146

Downbeat, 72

Duberman, Martin, *Paul Robeson*, 152

Dunaway, David King: *How Can I Keep from Singing? The Ballad of Pete Seeger*, 10, 152; *Singing Out: An Oral History of America's Folk Music Revivals*, 10

Duncan, Laura, NAACP concert flyer, 66

Dunson, Josh, *Freedom in the Air: Song Movements of the Sixties*, 124, 156

Dyer-Bennet, Richard, 9, 153; *The 20th Century Minstrel*, 53; Town Hall concert flyer, 44

Dylan, Bob, 9; career, 155; Carnegie Chapter Hall concert notice, 105; *Dont Look Back*, 146; first concert hall appearance, 155; "Mr. Tambourine Man" sheet music, 138; *Saturday Evening Post* cover, 121; *Sing Out!* cover, 1962, 98; *The Times They Are a-Changin'*, 138

Easy Riders, 154

Edwards, Jay, *The Coffee House Songbook*, 126

Elektra Folk Song Kit, 82

Elektra Records, 154

Ella Jenkins Song Book for Children, The, 135

Escaping the Delta: Robert Johnson and the Invention of the Blues, 12

Ethnic and Border Music: A Regional Exploration, 12

ethnic music, 8

"Eve of Destruction" sheet music, 138

Ewan MacColl Peggy Seeger Songbook, 135

Exploring American Folk Music: Ethnic, Grassroots, and Regional Traditions in the United States, 12

Face of Folk Music, The, 11, 130, 156

Famous Cowboy Songs and Mountain Ballads, 18

Favorite American Union Songs, 48

Festival movie poster, 147

field recordings, authenticity, 9

Filene, Benjamin, *Romancing the Folk: Public Memory and American Roots Music*, 12

films, 155, 156

Fireside Book of Folk Songs, 53, 153

Fisher, Dave, "Cotton Fields" sheet music, 138

Flatt & Scruggs, 155; concert flyer, 119

Folk Artists '69, magazine covering 1969 Newport Folk Festival, 147

folk books, 156

Folk City: New York and the American Folk Music Revival, 11

folk clubs, 154

folk festivals, popularity, 154

Folk Forum, 147

folk magazines, 156; local, 156

folk music: commercial promotion, 7, 9; defined, 7; distribution, 8; origins, 8; promotional formats, 9; scope, 8

Folk Music, 123

Folk Music: A Regional Exploration, 12

folk music concerts, 154

Folk Music for Hazard, Kentucky, coal miners program, 1965, 107

Folk Music Guide USA, 90

Folk Music magazine, 155

Folk Music: The Basics, 10

Folk Music USA, 87

"Folk Rock Is a Drag" advertisement for Hagstrom Guitars featuring Frank Zappa, 136

Folk Scene, The, 141

"Folk Singers Wear Wranglers" *Life* magazine advertisement, 101

Folk Song Book, The, 69

Folk Song Jamboree, 95

Folk Songs at Columbia University with Tom Glazer et al., concert flyer, 90

Folk Songs of America and Other Lands, 66

Folk Songs of Peggy Seeger, 129

Folk Today!, 124

Folklore Center, 105, 154; concert flyer, 90

folk-rock, 8, 156

Folksing, 95

Folksingers Guild, Folkmusic at Midnight concert flyer, 90

folksong books, 155

Folk-Song Symphony, 20

Folkway Concert Series, New York flyer, 91

Folkways Records, 13; catalog for Pete Seeger, 82

"For the Love of Pete and Freedom" flyer, 105

"Four Approaches to Folk Song" program, University of California, Berkeley, 1958, 84

14 Traditional Spanish Songs from Texas, 47

Fox, Oscar, 152

Frank Warner Sings American Folk Songs and Ballads, 70

Freedom in the Air: Song Movements of the Sixties, 124

Freedom Singers, 155; concert program, 119
Friedman, Samuel H., *Rebel Song Book*, 28
Friends of Old Time Music, 155; concert flyer, 97, 118
Friesen, Gordon, 155

Gahr, David, *The Face of Folk Music*, 11, 130, 156
Gardyloo (folk magazine), 79, 154
Garland of Mountain Song, A, 69
Gateway Singers, 154
Geer, Will, concert flyer for *Broadside* fundraiser, 118
Gellert, Lawrence, 152; *Negro Songs of Protest*, 24
George-Warren, Holly, *American Roots Music*, 10
Gerberg, Mort, *Hootenanny* cartoons, 112
Gerdes Folk City, New York, 155; concert schedule, 90
Gibson, Bob, 154
Gilbert, Ronnie, 153
Gilkyson, Terry, "Marianne," 59
Gilliland, Henry, 9
Git On Board: Folk Songs for Group Singing, 53
Glazer, Ray, "Round the Same Merry Go Round" (Wallace campaign record), 51
Glazer, Tom, 152, 153; *Favorite American Union Songs*, 48; Folk Songs at Columbia University concert flyer, 1960, 91; "Libby's Tomato Juice Song," 51; *A New Treasury of Folk Songs*, 95; "Old Soldiers Never Die," 59
"Go 'Way from My Window," 41
Goehring, George, "Hootenanny" sheet music, 112
Goldblatt, Burt, *The Country Music Story*, 124
Goldsmith, Peter, *Making People's Music: Moe Asch and Folkways Records*, 153
Gone to the Country: The New Lost City Ramblers and the Folk Music Revival, 10
"Goodnight, Irene," 56, 153
Gordo comic strip, 1962, 98, 155
Gordon, Robert Winslow, 8
gospel tunes, 8
Grafman, Howard, *Folk Music USA*, 87
Green, Douglas B., *Singing in the Saddle: The History of the Singing Cowboy*, 151
Greenback Dollar: The Incredible Rise of the Kingston Trio, 11
Greenbrier Boys, 79, 107, 154
Greenwich Village Story, 92

Grenell, Horace, *The Young People's Records Folk Song Book*, 55
Guard, Dave, 154
Guthrie, Arlo, 156; "Alice's Restaurant" sheet music, 149; Masonic Temple concert flyer, 142
Guthrie, Jack, "Oklahoma Hills," 40, 153
Guthrie, Woody, 9, 66, 152; *American Folksong*, 34; *Ballads of Sacco & Vanzetti*, 103; *Born to Win*, 124; *Bound for Glory*, 37, 152; death, 155; "A Guy Is a Guy," 59; "The Gypsy Rover" sheet music, 138; *Hard Hitting Songs for Hard-Hit People*, 128, 156; health, 154; launch of People's Songs, 153; *Midnight Special*, 33; "Oklahoma Hills," 40; "This Land Is Your Land" sheet music, 138

Hajdu, David, *Positively 4th Street: The Lives and Times of Joan Baez, Bob Dylan, Mimi Baez Fariña and Richard Fariña*, 155
"Halleluiah! I'm a Bum," 16
Hamilton, Marybeth, *In Search of the Blues: Black Voices, White Visions*, 12
Harburg, E. Y., "I've Got a Ballot," 51
Hard Hitting Songs for Hard-Hit People, 128, 156
Harris, Roy, *Folk-Song Symphony*, 20
Harry Belafonte: His Complete Life Story, 77
Haufrect, Herbert, *Folksing*, 95
Hawes, Baldwin, 152
Hawes, Bess, 152
Hays, Lee, 152, 153; "If I Had a Hammer," 155; "If I Had a Hammer" sheet music, 103
"Hear America Singing with Guy Carawan," 66
Hellerman, Fred, 153
Hester, Carolyn, *Saturday Evening Post* cover, 121
Highlander Folk School benefit program, 45
Highwaymen, 154; *Folk Song Album*, 87
hillbilly ballads, 152
hillbilly recordings, 8–9, 152–53
"Hill-Billy 'Round-Up' Songbook, The," 26
Hille, Waldemar, *The People's Song Book*, 59
History of Folk Music Festivals in the United States, A, 10–11
Hit Parader, December 1963, 136
Hobo in Song and Poetry, The, 16
hobos, 151
Holzman, Jac, 154
"Hoot!" Ash Grove flyer, 1963, 107

"Hoot" Kit! Song Book, 113
hootenanny: commercial use of, 108, 155; defined, 155
Hootenanny: cartoons, 1964, 112; magazine, March 1964, 112; magazine, May 1964, 113
Hootenanny (ABC-TV) merchandise, 108–9
Hootenanny at Carnegie Hall, 1961, 63
hootenanny craze of 1964, 9
Hootenanny Hoot: advertisement, 116; movie lobby card, 1963, 113; movie poster, 1963, 112, 116
Hootenanny Hotshots, 110
"Hootenanny" sheet music, 112–13
Hootenanny Sing! music book, 114
Hootenanny Song Book: Reprints from Sing Out! The Folk Song Magazine, 114
Hootenanny Songs and Stars, 116
Hootenanny Tonight!, 114
Horther, Peg, "Hootenanny" sheet music, 112
Horton, Zilphia, *Labor Songs*, 28
"House I Live In, The," 41
Houston, Cisco, *Midnight Special*, 33
How Can I Keep from Singing? The Ballad of Pete Seeger, 10
How to Play the 5-String Banjo, 80
Huber, Patrick, *Linthead Stomp: The Creation of Country Music in the Piedmont South*, 12

I. W. W. Songs to Fan the Flames of Discontent, 14
I Wonder as I Wander: The Life of John Jacob Niles, 11
"If I Had a Hammer," 103, 155
"Immortal Negro Melodies: These Are Songs Paul Robeson Sings, The," 22
In Search of the Blues: Black Voices, White Visions, 12
Indiana University Folksong Club, 101
Industrial Workers of the World (IWW), 151
international cooperation, 153
international songs, 153
interracial movement, 153–54
Introducing American Folk Music, 12
Iron Men and Wooden Ships, 68
"Island in the Sun," 72
"I've Got a Ballot" (Wallace campaign record), 51
Ives, Burl, 9, 51, 152–53; "The Blue Tail Fly," 40; *Sea Songs*, 68; *The Wayfarin' Stranger* songbook, 53; *Wayfaring Stranger*, 47; *The Wayfaring Stranger* (accompanying booklet), 38

Jefferson Chorus: "Solidarity Forever," 48; "Union Maid," 48
Jenkins, Paul, *Richard Dyer-Bennet: The Last Minstrel*, 10, 153
Jim & Jean, 107
Joan Baez Songbook, The, 125
Joe Hill movie poster, 149
John Hancock Hall concert flyer, 1965, 107
"John Henry," 22
Josh White Guitar Method, The, 80
Journeymen, 154; songbook, 87

Kaufman, Will: *Singing for Peace: Antiwar Songs in American History*, 156; *Woody Guthrie: American Radical*, 10, 152
Kelley, Robert, *The Coffee House Songbook*, 126
Kent, Rockwell, 45
"Kentucky Wonder Bean, The," 27
Kindergarten Book of Folk-Songs, A, 16
Kingston Trio, 9, 154; on *Life* magazine cover, 87; "The M.T.A.," 61; on *Rogue* magazine cover, 87; "A Worried Man," 61
Kingston Trio, The, 98
Kolb, John, *A Treasury of Folk Songs*, 69
Kolb, Sylvia, *A Treasury of Folk Songs*, 69
Krehbiel, Henry Edward, *Afro-American Folksongs: A Study in Racial and National Music*, 14

labor songbooks, 8, 152
Labor Songs, 28
labor union songs, 9
labor unions, 151, 152, 153
Lampell, Millard, 152
Lancelot, Sir, "Walk in Peace" poster, 132
Landeck, Beatrice: *Git On Board: Folk Songs for Group Singing*, 53; interest in children's music, 153; *More Songs to Grow On*, 55; *Songs to Grow On*, 55
Larkin, Margaret, 151; *Singing Cowboy: A Book of Western Songs*, 19
Lead Belly, 8, 21, 151–52; Highlander Folk School benefit, 45; *Negro Sinful Songs*, 32
Lead Belly, Woody Guthrie, and Cisco Huston, *Midnight Special*, 33
Lead Belly and the Golden Gate Quartet, *"The Midnight Special" and Other Southern Prison Songs*, 32

Leadbelly Legend, The, 89

Leadbelly movie poster, 149

Leadbelly Songbook, The, 128

Leary, James P., *Polkabilly: How the Goose Island Ramblers Redefined American Folk Music*, 12

"Leaving on a Jet Plane" sheet music, 138

Ledbetter, Huddie, 151. *See also* Lead Belly

Ledgin, Stephanie P., *Discovering Folk Music*, 12

left-wing politics, 153, 155

Legend of Tom Dooley, The, 92

Leisy, James F., *Hootenanny Tonight!*, 114

LeMon, Melvin, 152; *The Miner Sings*, 25

Lennon Sisters, *TV, Radio, Movie Reporter* cover, 121

Lester Flatt & Earl Scruggs with the Foggy Mountain Boys, 126

Let's All Sing . . . Calypso, 75

Leventhal, Harold, press release, 1963, 105

Lewine, Richard, "Hootenanny Saturday Night" sheet music, 113

"Libby's Tomato Juice Song," 51

Library of Congress: Archive of American Folk Song, 7–8; "Folk Music of the United States" series, 8; as issuer of albums, 8

Lift Every Voice! The Second People's Song Book, 59

Limeliters, 154

Linthead Stomp: The Creation of Country Music in the Piedmont South, 12

"Little Boxes" sheet music, 138

Little Sandy Review (folk magazine), 79, 154

Lomax, Alan, 151, 152, 153; albums from field recordings, 8; *American Ballads and Folk Songs*, 8, 24; *American Folk Guitar*, 80; on authenticity, 9; *Best Loved American Folk Songs*, 47; *Cowboy Songs and Other Frontier Ballads*, 19; fieldwork, 7; *14 Traditional Spanish Songs from Texas*, 47; *Hard Hitting Songs for Hard-Hit People*, 128, 156; "I've Got a Ballot" (Wallace campaign record), 51; *The Leadbelly Legend*, 89; *The Leadbelly Songbook*, 128; *Negro Folk Songs as Sung by Lead Belly*, 22; *Our Singing Country*, 8; *Punch* cartoon, 150

Lomax, John A., 7, 151, 152, 153; *Adventures of a Ballad Hunter*, 47; *American Ballads and Folk Songs*, 8, 24; on authenticity, 9; *Best Loved American Folk Songs*, 47; *Cowboy Songs*, 19; *Cowboy Songs and Other Frontier Ballads*, 19; *14 Traditional Spanish Songs from Texas*, 47; *The Leadbelly Legend*, 89; *Negro Folk Songs as Sung by Lead Belly*, 22

Lomax, Ruby T., *14 Traditional Spanish Songs from Texas*, 47

Lonesome Valley (album), 152

Lonesome Valley: A Collection of American Folk Music, 37

Long, Burt, "Cindy, Oh Cindy," 59

Lopez, Trini, 155

Lornell, Kip: *Exploring American Folk Music: Ethnic, Grassroots, and Regional Traditions in the United States*, 12; *Introducing American Folk Music*, 12; *The Life and Legend of Leadbelly*, 152; *The NPR Curious Listener's Guide to American Folk Music*, 12

Love Diary, 111

Luboff, Norman, *Songs of Man*, 126

Lunsford, Bascom Lamar, *30 and 1 Folk Songs from the Southern Mountains*, 16

MacColl, Ewan, 155; *Ewan MacColl Peggy Seeger Songbook*, 135; Town Hall concert flyer, 118

Maguire, Leo, "The Gypsy Rover" sheet music, 138

Mairants, Ivor, *The Josh White Guitar Method*, 80

Malone, Bill, *Music from the True Vine: Mike Seeger's Life and Musical Journey*, 10

Manhattan Chorus, "On the Picket Line," 48

Manning, B. T., *Folk Music USA*, 87

Marais, Josef: "A-Round the Corner," 59; *Songs from the Veld*, 42

Marais & Miranda: *Folk Song Jamboree*, 95; *World Folk Songs*, 95

"Marianne," 59

Marianne and Other Calypso Songs You'll Like, 75

Matthews, J. B., "The Commies Go After Kids" cartoon, 65

Mazor, Barry, *Ralph Peer and the Making of Popular Roots Music*, 151

McBirnie, William Steuart, *Songs of Subversion*, 110

McClintock, Harry "Mac," "Halleluiah! I'm a Bum," 16

McDonald, Country Joe, *Rag Baby*, 156

McDougal, Dennis, *Dylan: The Biography*, 155

McGhee, Brownie, 70, 154, 156; Highlander Folk School benefit, 45; Vanilla Fudge postcard, 142

McNeill, Don, 51

Midnight Special, 33

"Midnight Special, The," and Other Southern Prison Songs, 32

"Midnight Special, The" concert, Carnegie Hall, 63

Miller, Frank, "Marianne," 59

Miller, Karl Hagstrom, 9; *Segregating Sound: Inventing Folk and Pop Music in the Age of Jim Crow*, 12

Miner Sings, The, 25

mining songs, 152

minstrel tunes, 8

Mississippi John Hurt: His Life, His Times, His Blues, 10

"Mit Gezang Tzum Kamf," 20

Mitchell Trio Song Book, The, 127

Mix, Tom, 151; *Western Songs*, 18

More Songs to Grow On, 55

Morse, Jim, *The Dell Book of Great American Folk Songs*, 95

Mountain Songs, 26

Moyer, Harvey P., *Songs of Socialism*, 14

"Mr. Tambourine Man" sheet music, 138

"Murderous Minstrel," 20

Muse of Parker Street: More Songs by Malvina Reynolds, The, 135

Music from the True Vine: Mike Seeger's Life and Musical Journey, 10

"My Bonnie Lies over the Ocean" (Wheates Red Record), 65

"My Song Is My Weapon": People's Songs, American Communism, and the Politics of Culture, 1930–1950, 153

Negro dialect ditties, 9

Negro Folk Music U.S.A., 87

Negro Sinful Songs, 32

Negro Songs of Protest, 24

Nemiroff, Bob, 59

New American Songbag, 69

New Lost City Ramblers, 155

New Lost City Ramblers & Elizabeth Cotton, concert flyer, 1960, 97

New Lost City Ramblers Song Book, The, 128

New Masses concert notices, 45

New Treasury of Folk Songs, A, 95

Newport Folk Festival, 155, 156; beginning, 154; *Folk Artists '69* magazine, 148; program, 1959, 84; program, 1960, 105; program, 1971, 149; programs, 1964, 1966, 1967, 145

Newport Folk Festival Songbook, The, 130

Niles, John Jacob, 9, 152, 153; *The Anglo-American Ballad Study Book*, 41; "Go 'Way from My Window," 41; *More Songs of the Hill-Folk*, 27; *Songs of the Hill-Folk*, 27

900 Miles: The Ballads, Blues and Folksongs of Cisco Houston, 128

No. 1 Folk Song Album, The, 127

Noebel, David A., *Rhythm, Riots and Revolution*, 110

Norman Luboff Choir, "Calypso Carnival," 75

Now Sound of Folk Music, The, 146

NPR Curious Listener's Guide to American Folk Music, The, 12

Oak Publications, 156

Ochs, Phil, 9, 107, 155; concert flyer, 118

Odetta: Recorded Folk Songs, 122

"Oklahoma Hills," 40, 153

Old Familiar Tunes and Race Records, 38

Old Favorite Songs, 14

"Old Soldiers Never Die," 59

"On the Picket Line," 48

"On Top of Old Smoky," 40, 65

100 Books Every Folk Music Fan Should Own, 13

One Hundred English Folksongs, 14

140 Folk-Songs: Rote Songs for Grades I, II, and III, 16

104 Folk Songs as Recorded on Folkways Records by Famous Folk Song Singers, 127

"One Meat Ball," 41

Orange Crush Hootenanny Party Kit, 114

Oscar Brand's Authentic Hootenanny Song Book, 108

Our Singing Country, 8

Palmer-Hughes *Hootenanny* accordion instruction book, 114

Paul Clayton and the Folksong Revival, 10

Paxton, Tom, 107

peace movement, 132–33, 134, 152, 156

Pen, Ron, *I Wonder as I Wander: The Life of John Jacob Niles*, 11, 152

Pennebaker, D. A., *Dont Look Back*, 146

"People for Peace Concert," 1965, 132

People's Song Book, The, 59

People's Songs: beginnings, 153; Hootenanny flyer, 45

People's Songs (publication), 49

Pete Seeger On Record, 147

Pete Seeger Reader, The, 11

Peter, Paul and Mary: "Blowin' in the Wind" ad in *Billboard*, 105; *Cosmopolitan* cover, 121; *Hootenanny* cover, 1963, 113; "If I Had a Hammer," 155

Peter, Paul and Mary on Tour, 98

Peterson, Walter, "The Kentucky Wonder Bean," 27

Petrus, Stephen, *Folk City: New York and the American Folk Music Revival*, 11, 155

Philadelphia Folk Festival, 156; program, 1966, 1967, 145

Play and Sing: America's Greatest Collection of Old Time Songs and Mountain Ballads, 26

political songs, 8, 9, 152, 153

Polkabilly: How the Goose Island Ramblers Redefined American Folk Music, 12

Pop Folk, 147

pop folk music, 8

"Popular Ballads and Mountaineer Tunes," 16

Popular Cowboy Songs, 30

popular magazines featuring folk performers, 155

Porterfield, Nolan, *Last Cavalier: The Life and Times of John Lomax, 1867–1948*, 151

Poulin, A., Jr., *The American Folk Scene: Dimensions of the Folksong Revival*, 130

Preachin' the Blues: The Life and Times of Son House, 10

Progressive Party, 153

protest songs, 152, 156

race records, 8–9, 152–53

radical movements, 151, 153

radical songbooks, 152

radical songs, 152

Rag Baby, 136, 156

"Rain: A Negro Folk Song Collected by the Misses Turner," 14

Rainbow Quest: The Folk Music Revival and American Society, 1940–1970, 10

"Rally for Trade and Peace with China," 63

Ramblin' Boy and Other Songs by Tom Paxton, 129

Ramblin' Jack Elliott: The Never-Ending Highway, 11

Rand School Press, 152

Ratcliffe, Philip R., *Mississippi John Hurt: His Life, His Times, His Blues*, 10

Rebel Song Book, 28

records: formats, 9; history, 8–9

Red Channels: The Report of Communist Influence in Radio and Television, 65, 154

Red Song Book, 28

Reds, Whites, and Blues: Social Movements, Folk Music, and Race in the United States, 10

Reed, Susan, 9

Reineke, Hank: *Arlo Guthrie: The Warner/Reprise Years*, 11; *Ramblin' Jack Elliott: The Never-Ending Highway*, 11

Reuss, JoAnne C., *American Folk Music and Left-Wing Politics, 1927–1957*, 151

Reuss, Richard A., *American Folk Music and Left-Wing Politics, 1927–1957*, 151

Reynolds, Malvina, 154, 155; concert flyer for *Broadside* fundraiser, 118; "Little Boxes" sheet music, 138; *The Muse of Parker Street: More Songs by Malvina Reynolds*, 135; *Song in My Pocket*, 70; "What Have They Done to the Rain?" sheet music, 138

Reynolds, Nick, 154

Rhythm, Riots and Revolution, 110

Richard Dyer-Bennet: The Last Minstrel, 10, 153

Riesman, Bob, *I Feel So Good: The Life and Times of Big Bill Broonzy*, 10

Rinzler, Ralph, 155

Ritchie, Jean, *A Garland of Mountain Song*, 69

Robertson, Eck, 9

Robeson, Paul, 152, 153; concert flyer, Fresno Memorial Auditorium, 45; Highlander Folk School benefit program, 45; "John Henry," 22

Robinson, Earl, "The House I Live In," 41

Rock Folk Song Folio, 136

Rock Folk Songs, 136

Roll the Union On, 48

Romancing the Folk: Public Memory and American Roots Music, 12

Rome, Harold J., *10 New Songs the Soviets Sing*, 42

Rooftop Singers, "Tom Cat" sheet music, 138

roots music described, 7

Roots of the Revival: American and British Folk Music in the 1950s, 11

Rosenberg, Neil V., *Transforming Tradition: Folk Music Revivals Examined*, 12
"Round the Same Merry Go Round" (Wallace campaign record), 51
Rounder Records, 12
"Roving Kind, The," 61
Roy, William G., *Reds, Whites, and Blues: Social Movements, Folk Music, and Race in the United States*, 10
rural songs, 151
Rush, Tom, Town Hall concert flyer, 118

Sainte-Marie, Buffy, 107
San Diego Folk Festival program, 1967, 145
Sandburg, Carl, 7, 151, 152; *The American Songbag*, 8, 16, 154; *New American Songbag*, 69
Sanders, Betty, People's Songs Hootenanny, 45
Santelli, Robert: *American Roots Music*, 10; *This Land Is Your Land: Woody Guthrie and the Journey of an American Folksong*, 11
Schaeffer, Jacob, "Mit Gezang Tzum Kamf," 20
Schaum, John W., *The Folk Song Book*, 69
Schirmer's American Folk-Song Series, 41
Scott, Tom, *Sing of America*, 47
Scully, Michael, *The Never-Ending Revival: Rounder Records and the Folk Alliance*, 156
sea shanties, 8
sea songs, 68, 154
Sea Songs, 68
2nd Fret, Philadelphia, 140
Seeger, Peggy, 155; *American Folk Guitar*, 80; *Ewan MacColl Peggy Seeger Songbook*, 135; Town Hall concert flyer, 118
Seeger, Pete, 9, 152, 153, 154, 156; banjo instruction book, 154; Folkways Records catalog, 82; *Hard Hitting Songs for Hard-Hit People*, 128, 156; *How to Play the 5-String Banjo*, 80; "If I Had a Hammer," 155; "If I Had a Hammer" sheet music, 103; "The Midnight Special" concert, Carnegie Hall, 63; Mt. Tamolpais concert flyer, 142; NAACP concert flyer, 66; in the 1970s, 156; People's Songs Hootenanny, 45
Seeger, Ruth Crawford: *American Folk Songs for Children*, 55; interest in children's music, 153
Shane, Bob, 154
Shanty Boys, 154; *Caravan* cover, 78

Shantymen and Shantyboys, 68
Sharp, Cecil J., 7, 151; *One Hundred English Folksongs*, 14
Shay, Frank, *American Sea Songs & Chanteys*, 68
sheet music, 156; history, 151
Shelton, Robert: *Born to Win*, 124; *The Country Music Story*, 124; *The Face of Folk Music*, 11, 130, 156
Siegmeister, Elie, *Work and Sing*, 42
Silber, Irwin, 103, 153; *Lift Every Voice! The Second People's Song Book*, 59; as owner of Oak Publications, 156
Sinatra, Frank, 153; "Goodnight, Irene," 56
"Sing-In for Peace," Carnegie Hall concert flyer, 132
Sing of America, 47
Sing Out!, 57, 59; February–March 1966, 136; "Frets and Frails" column, 154; Carnegie Hall hootenanny program, 1958, 84; Carnegie Hall hootenanny program, 1961, 63; July 1951, December 1953, 59; May 1950, 103, 153, 155; October–November 1962, 98; September 1965, 136; Summer 1959, 57
Sing Out, Sweet Land (accompanying booklet), 38
Singer, Lou, "One Meat Ball," 41
Singing Cowboy: A Book of Western Songs, 19
Singing for Peace: Antiwar Songs in American History, 11, 156
Singing Out: An Oral History of America's Folk Music Revivals, 10
16: Elvis vs. Belafonte, 65
16 magazine, 154
skiffle music, 154
Skiffle: The Story of Folk Song with a Jazz Beat, 89
Sky, Patrick, 107
Slave Songs of the United States, 7
Sloan, P. F., "Eve of Destruction" sheet music, 138
Smith, Harry, 153; *Anthology of American Folk Music* booklet, 57
Smith, Judith, *Becoming Belafonte: Black Artist, Public Radical*, 154
Smithsonian-Folkways, 153
"So Long, It's Been Good to Know Yuh," 59, 61
Socialist Party, 152
"Solidarity Forever," 48
song folios defined, 152
Song Hits Magazine, 136
Song in My Pocket, 70

songbooks, history, 8, 151
Songmakers Almanac, The, 141, 156
Songs for John Doe, 37, 45
Songs for Peace, 135
Songs from the Ash Grove, 89
Songs from the Veld, 42
Songs of Citizen CIO, 48
Songs of Early America, The (accompanying booklet), 38
Songs of Man, 126
Songs of Phil Ochs, 128
Songs of Socialism, 14
Songs of Subversion, 110
Songs of the Almanac Singers, 37
Songs of the Lincoln Brigade, 34
Songs of the People, 28
Songs of the Plains, 30
Songs of the Range, 19
"Songs of Woody Guthrie, The" flyer, 66
Songs to Grow On, 55
songsters defined, 8
Sorrels, Rosalie, concert flyer for *Broadside* fundraiser, 118
Spencer, Scott B., *The Ballad Collectors of North America: How Gathering Folksongs Transformed Academic Thought and American Identity*, 12
spirituals, 8, 151
Spoelstra, Mark, concert flyer for *Broadside* fundraiser, 118
Star Calypso Songs, 77
Stinson Asch Record catalog, 38
Stoneman Family concert flyer, University of Illinois Campus Folksong Club, 101
Stracke, Win, *Songs of Man*, 126
Strange Fruit, 32
Stray Notes, 141, 156
Stringfield, Lamar, *30 and 1 Folk Songs from the Southern Mountains*, 16
Student Peace Union, *Songs for Peace*, 135
Students for a Democratic Society "People for Peace Concert," 132
Surette, Thomas Whitney, *140 Folk-Songs: Rote Songs for Grades I, II, and III*, 16
Szwed, John, *Alan Lomax: The Man Who Recorded the World*, 10, 152

"Taking It Easy," 61
Talkin' 'Bout a Revolution: Music and Social Change in America, 11
Talking Union, 48
Tarriers, 154; *Calypso-Land*, 75
Teen magazine, 65, 154
10 New Songs the Soviets Sing, 42
Terry, Sonny, 156; Highlander Folk School benefit, 45
Terry, Sonny, and Brownie McGhee: concert flyer, ca. 1966, 142; Vanilla Fudge postcard, 143
Testimonial to Rockwell Kent, concert notice, 45
Textile Workers Union, 152
30 and 1 Folk Songs from the Southern Mountains, 16
"This Land Is Your Land" sheet music, 138
This Land Is Your Land: Woody Guthrie and the Journey of an American Folksong, 11
Thomas, Jean, *Ballad Makin' in the Mountains of Kentucky*, 129
Three Cowboy Desperado Songs, 25
"3 Great Philco Radio Shows: Bing Crosby, Don McNeill, Burl Ives," 51
Times They Are a-Changin', The, 138
Tin Pan Alley tunes, 9
Tiny Texan, *World's Greatest Collection of Cowboy and Mountain Ballads*, 18
"Tom Cat" sheet music, 138
"Tom Dooley," 61, 154
Tommy Sands vs. Belafonte and Elvis, 77
Transforming Tradition: Folk Music Revivals Examined, 12
Treasure Chest of Homespun Songs, 27
Treasury of Folk Songs, A, 69
Tune Up (folk magazine), 156; December 1963, 136
Turner, Gil, concert flyer for *Broadside* fundraiser, 118
20th Century Minstrel, The, 53
"Tzena, Tzena, Tzena," 61

UCLA Folk Music Festival, program, 1963, 145
Uhry, Alfred, "Hootenanny Saturday Night" sheet music, 113
"Union Maid," 48
University of California, Berkeley: "American Balladry and Folk Song" program, 84; "Four Approaches to Folk Song" program, 84; notice

of concerts, Fall 1962, March 1963, 97, 101; "A Weekend of Folk Music" program, 84
University of Illinois Campus Folksong Club, 101
urban-based folk musicians, 9
urban songs, 151

Van Ronk, Dave: Indiana University Folksong Club concert, 1964, 155; Indiana University Folksong Club concert flyer, 1964, 101; *The Mayor of MacDougal Street: A Memoir*, 155
Vanilla Fudge postcard, 142
Vega Banjo ad for "Seeger Model," 80, 154
Victor recordings, 151
Victor Records flyer, 1957, 16
Victorian parlor songs, 8, 9
Village Stompers at Washington Square, The, 122
von Schmidt, Eric, *Come for to Sing*, 135

Wade, Stephen, *The Beautiful Music All Around Us: Field Recordings and the American Experience*, 12
Wald, Elijah: *Escaping the Delta: Robert Johnson and the Invention of the Blues*, 12; *John White: Society Blues*, 152; *The Mayor of MacDougal Street: A Memoir*, 155
"Walk in Peace" poster, 132
Wallace, Henry, 153; campaign records, 51
Walt Disney's Ballad of Davy Crockett: Hootenanny Song Album, 126
Warner, Frank, 70, 154
Warner, Lorraine d'Oremieulx, *A Kindergarten Book of Folk-Songs*, 16
Waters, Muddy, 8
Watson, Doc: Indiana University Folksong Club concert, 1965, 155; Indiana University Folksong Club concert flyer, 1965, 101
Wayfarin' Stranger songbook, 53
Wayfaring Stranger, 47
Wayfaring Stranger, The (accompanying booklet), 38
WBAI Club concert flyer, 119
We Shall Overcome: Songs of the Southern Freedom Movement, 135
Weavers, 9, 154, 155; *The Cash Box* cover, 59; concert flyer, Berkeley, 1962, 101; concert flyer, Berkeley, 1963, 101; *Folk Songs of America and Other Lands*, 66; "Goodnight, Irene," 56, 153; influence on other groups, 154; "The Roving Kind," 61; *Sing Folk Songs of America and Other Lands*, 66; "So Long, It's Been Good to Know Yuh," 61; "Taking It Easy," 61; "Tom Dooley," 61; Town Hall Concerts, 63; "Tzena, Tzena, Tzena," 61; "When the Saints Go Marching In," 60; "Wimoweh," 61
Weavers at Rotary Ann Day, The, 63
Weavers' Song Book, The, 126
"Weekend of Folk Music, A" program, University of California, Berkeley, 1958, 84
Weissman, Dick: *100 Books Every Folk Music Fan Should Own*, 12; *Talkin' 'Bout a Revolution: Music and Social Change in America*, 11; *Which Side Are You On? An Inside History of the Folk Music Revival in America*, 10
West, Hedy: concert notice, 119; University of Illinois Campus Folksong Club concert flyer, 101
western songs, 8, 152
Western Songs, 18
"What Have They Done to the Rain?" sheet music, 138
"When the Saints Go Marching In," 60
Which Side Are You On? An Inside History of the Folk Music Revival in America, 10
White, Josh, 9, 152, 153; "John Henry," 22; *The Josh White Guitar Method*, 80; Orchestra Hall concert program, 45; promo advertisement, 34; *Strange Fruit*, 32
White Top Folk Festival, Virginia, 152; flyer, 22
Whittier, Henry, 9
Wicken, Wally, "Goodnight, Irene," 56
Wilgus, D. K., *Anglo-American Folksong Scholarship since 1898*, 12, 65, 154
"Wimoweh," 61
Wolfe, Bill, "Round the Same Merry Go Round" (Wallace campaign record), 51
Wolfe, Charles, *The Life and Legend of Leadbelly*, 151
Woody Guthrie: American Radical, 10
Work, John W., *American Negro Songs and Spirituals*, 20
Work and Sing, 42
Work and Sing: A History of Occupational and Labor Songs in the United States, 11
work songs, 153
Workers Song Book, 20, 151
World's Greatest Collection of Cowboy and Mountain Ballads, 18

Worlds of Sound: The Story of Smithsonian Folkways, 10
"Worried Man, A," 61
WWVA World's Original Radio Jamboree Famous Songs, 34
Wynne, Ben, *In Tune: Charley Patton, Jimmie Rodgers, and the Roots of American Music*, 151

Young, Israel G., 155; catalog, 82; Folk Music Guide USA, 90; Folklore Center, 90, 154; "Frets and Frails" column, 154; as sponsor of Dylan concert, 155
Young Folk Song Book, 127
Young People's Records, 153
Young People's Records Folk Song Book, The, 55
Young Swingers, The, 92

Zack, Ian, *Say No to the Devil: The Life and Musical Genius of Rev. Gary Davis*, 155
Zaret, Hy, "One Meat Ball," 41
Zimmerman, Robert, 155